D1528210

Holistic
Enterprise Architecture
for
Mergers and Acquisitions

Scott A. Bernard

authorHOUSE

AuthorHouse™
1663 Liberty Drive
Bloomington, IN 47403
www.authorhouse.com
Phone: 833-262-8899

Published by AuthorHouse 01/06/2023

ISBN: 978-1-6655-7979-7 (sc)
ISBN: 978-1-6655-7978-0 (e)

Library of Congress Control Number: 2023900350

Print information available on the last page.

Contents

Contents

About the Author

Scott A. Bernard grew up in Southern California and has worked in the public, private, military, and academic sectors. His is a retired naval aviator and active college professor who enjoys sailing, traveling, and time with family. Dr. Bernard has served in a wide range of staff, management, and executive positions during the past half-century, including starting as a grocery store bagger, then after college as an accounting supervisor, naval officer and patrol plane pilot, college professor, computer manager, government executive, business consultant, and father of three wonderful children. These experiences and global travels have shaped his views and teaching approach.

Dedication

My children are my pride and joy.
Thank you to Bill, Kristin, and Katie for being
such wonderful, loving people.

Let's Avoid Buzzwords/Buzz Phrases

(I will try to use plain language instead of the following terms)

Advertainment, agile, back channel, bandwidth, best practice, big data, bleeding edge, blue sky, boil the ocean, business intelligence, buy-in, circle back, circle of trust, cloud, cognitive dissonance, customer journey, data-driven-decision-making, devops, disruptor, dive, digitization, drill down, ducks in a row, ecosystem, empower, engagement, frenemy, full plate, ghost, governance, green field, hyper local, ideate, in-the-weeds, incentivize, influencer, internet of things, leverage, low hanging fruit, machine learning, move the needle, narrative arc, net-net, new normal, on your radar, re-frame, open the kimono, opex/capex, optics, pain point, paradigm shift, ping, pivot, playbook, quick win, reframe, rightsized, road kill, single pane of glass, reskill, rockstar, same sheet of music, socialize, synergy, swim lane, take this offline, think outside the box, thought leader, time suck, transformation, unpack, user experience, value chain, verticals, virtual, and win-win.

Introduction

The word "organization" is defined by the Cambridge Dictionary as "*a group of people who work together for a shared purpose in a continuing way*." The word can also mean "*the way in which something is arranged*." Both of these definitions are foundational to the concepts presented in this book, which center on how to create a new effective organization from the melding of two separate, often quite different, organizations.

Today's organizations are made up of people and things. It is the "things" side that is driving rapid change as artificial intelligence (AI) underpins more functions. *Understanding how modern organizations perform work with people and things* is especially important when you want to successfully combine two of them. The key word is *successfully*.

Business literature is full of examples of organizational mergers that did not go well. This book looks at reasons for this and suggests a way to do better. This book is not a text on advanced business, finance, or legal practices – those areas of mergers and acquisitions are well developed and usually not a cause of a failed merger. If you want detailed information on those areas, I suggest reading the textbook by Donald Depamphilis that is kept current and is very comprehensive.[1]

I use plain language and simple examples to show how organizations are not well understood and how the "pre-deal" and "post-deal" phases of mergers are often not done well. I will argue that this is due to an over-focus on financials and too little on retaining/engaging/blending key people and AI.

---

[1] DePamphilis, Donald (2021). *Mergers, Acquisitions, and Other Restructuring Activities: An Integrated Approach to Process, Tools, Cases, and Solutions* (11th Edition). Academic Press Publishing. ISBN-13-978-0128197820.

Organizations need to understand their structure and functions to be mission effective and cost efficient. A simple, intuitive approach to visualizing structure and function is helpful in achieving this understanding.

If you remember that in any organization goals drive activities, which are enabled by tools, then you can see the key relationships in the Holistic EA Framework. This model can be used with any type of organization and with multiple organizations.

In comparing multiple organizations, you need to use the same framework to have similar presentations of structure and functions. A holistic framework covers all aspects of an organization, which is important when enterprise-wide change and/or improvement is the objective.

In the case of mergers and acquisitions, two organizations are coming together. Even if some parts of either organization are not going to be part of the merger, that change to structure and function has to be understood and factored into other decisions. So, holistic views are needed, and HEA can help.

Mergers and acquisitions are big business in the private sector, lots of money is often involved. Unfortunately, the record of success in combining the organizations is not good. I think that this is because insufficient priority is given to understanding and documenting structure and function. Every organization changes all the time, so it is a moving target as you seek understanding. This makes it more difficult, but still doable if a HEA approach is used. If it is decided that such understanding is not needed, then you are flying blind.

Section 1

The Organization

1.1 Exists for a Reason

1.2 Has People and Things

1.3 Has Goals and Activities

1.4 Has an Architecture

Section 1

The Organization

This first section discusses the reason that organizations exist and important basic characteristics. The term "organization" is used as a noun and is defined as *"a group of people who work together for a shared purpose in a continuing way."*[2]

1.1 An Organization Exists for a Reason

There are two primary reasons that organizations exist:

- People are social and maintaining connections with others is important for physical and mental health.[3]
- People need and want things that they can't do, make, or obtain by themselves.

As a survival strategy, humans evolved into social animals who depend on others during their lifetime, especially in the early years. After that, dependency fades as a person gains in physical and mental capabilities, learns skills, and acquires resources. While humans are genetically predispositioned to be social creatures, you don't need others as much once you can cloth, feed, defend, and shelter yourself.

Hermits aside, most people embrace the company of others and the benefits of modern society. These benefits include comfortable houses, good healthcare, solid educations, rewarding jobs, and joining causes that improve the world.

Why do people work together and have a shared purpose? Because they want to or need to. Every person has basic needs for survival, and most have desires for a high standard of living and a better world. Some of these needs and desires can be attained and sustained through one's own efforts, but more often they are obtained through the capabilities of a group.

---

[2] CambridgeDictionary.com
[3] Source: cmha.ca/the-importance-of-human-connection/ (October 2019).

An interesting way to look at the reasons that organizations are established is to look at Abraham Maslow's *Hierarchy of Need"* model[4] (below) and other factors. This hierarchical model shows the primacy of needs to stay alive and safe, followed by basic needs to have social connectedness, and if those are met, to being the best you that is possible.

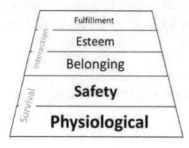

Other Factors
- Free Will
- Cultural Norms
- Personal Views

Often, the reason an organization is created is that the founder(s) have safety and/or social needs and feel that the best way to address that is to form a group that will be a stable source of what is needed (e.g., job, money, assets, ideas).

Why does it take a group to provide for needs and desires? Because resources and methods are often beyond the ability of one individual to obtain or utilize. While it is true that individuals with survival skills can maintain a basic existence, a healthier, more complete and comfortable life is attained through associations with groups, with their "give and take".

Groups that meet human needs and wants are essential to establishing and maintaining well-functioning societies and nations. That said, sustainable organizations can be difficult to create as they must be socially attractive, legally acceptable, and able to make a profit or collect sufficient fees or donations.

A legitimate, unifying reason must therefore be identified and communicated for an organization to become established, hold itself together, and allow for change when needed. Without such a reason, the organization will lose cohesion and commitment, become brittle, lose resources and customers, and eventually cease to exist.

---

[4] Maslow, A.H. (1943) A Theory of Human Motivation. *Psychological Review*, 50(4).

Beyond having a legitimate, unifying reason to establish the organization, it is important to remember that the government gets a vote. Government cares because it does not want organizations created that have values/objectives that are not consistent with those of the nation and localities – as codified in law and regulations.[5] That, and the public's ongoing (and growing) appetite for local/regional/national level services, is why taxation is needed and why approval is required for each organization to exist, beyond small social groups that do not conduct business nor condone illegality. Here is a scaled list:

Global Groups, Multinational Groups, Sovereign Nation-States, Government Agencies, Consortia, Corporations, Small Businesses, Non-Profits, Boards, Social Media, Clubs, Teams, Cliques, You

1.2 An Organization Has People and Things

An organization exists for a reason and must have government approval and resources (people and things) to operate. On the people side, there is a need for leadership, coordination, and execution skills. On the things side, there is a need for place(s) to work, tools and technology that support work, money, materials, ideas, and methods.

The resource mix changes as concepts and methods change. Many types of work can now be done remotely by people and tools connected globally in real time. One continuing trend that needs emphasis is that the role of people in many work processes continues to decrease as the capabilities of "smart" tools increases. The "smart" element is that which digitation (artificial intelligence - AI) provides in the form of computers, data, communication

---

[5] My view of world order is that laws, regulations, and policies derive their legitimacy through citizen/constituent approval and their power through laws and enforceability. Nation-states declare themselves to be legitimate and sovereign through proclamation or constitution – sometimes ratified by the population, sometimes not – and they declare that they will maintain their sovereignty through diplomacy, if possible, and by force if necessary. In these foundational documents, nations also often specify their own geographic boundaries, included ethnic groups, favored political, social, and religious groups, and principles for external relations and internal regulation. A nations' membership in international treaties and groups is non-mandatory, nor is the enforceability of the decisions of international groups, if the nation so chooses. As such, the nation-state is the highest-level organization of enduring consequence and international group cooperation is situational.

networks, digital assistants, search engines, mobile devices, information systems, peripherals. Software "bots" are programs that manage all or parts of a digitized work process. Robots perform mechanized work.

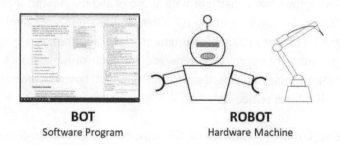

BOT
Software Program

ROBOT
Hardware Machine

Many of these tools incorporate AI elements that have been miniaturized, integrated, built-in, and may be swapable. I will refer to this human/ AI combination as "socio/techno". An example of this is "smart" farm equipment that can perform a variety of planting and harvesting tasks in an automated driverless mode using map coordinates for many land plots and being able to vary the amounts of materials being distributed based on soil, moisture, and pestilent conditions.

When investing in people and things, it is important for the organization to keep resiliency in mind because the future is unpredictable due to changing environmental conditions. An organization becomes strong and sustainable if positive and negative operating scenarios are developed and resource needs are extrapolated, which influences planning. One way to understand how an organization utilizes resources to achieve its mission is to use Michael Porter's "Value Chain" model[6] of activities, as shown below.

Support	Firm Infrastructure					Margin
	Human Resources Mgmt.					
	Technology					
	Procurement					
	Inbound Logistics	Operations	Outbound Logistics	Marketing & Sales	Service	

Primary Activities

---

[6] Porter, M (1965). *Competitive Advantage: Creating & Sustaining Superior Performance.*

The model depicts the process by which an organization's primary activities create a product or service, while support activities provide enabling resources. These support activities do not directly produce outputs, wo they are considered to be overhead costs that reduce the residual margin of profit or resources that can be repurposed.

1.3 An Organization Has Goals and Activities

Organizations exist for a reason, which is reflected in mission and vision statements that guide strategic and tactical goals, as well as the programs/projects that will achieve them. For example, a comprehensive health care organization forms in a rural community to bring all aspects of emergency, inpatient, and outpatient caregiving together at one location. As such, an effective mix of people, methods, and tools must be identified, resourced, implemented, maintained, and updated to meet the goal of effective holistic health care provision.

So, purpose generates goals. It would be nice if goals would then achieve themselves and not change over time. Unfortunately, goals do not achieve themselves and they do change in response to internal and external conditions, as well as changes in purpose that can come from different owners, key stakeholders, new regulations, and other influences.

Since goals do not achieve themselves just by speaking and publishing them, then activities are required. There are two general types of organizational activities: ongoing programs, and time-specific projects. Programs are intended to provide the oversight and resources that are needed to accomplish the work that produces goods and services on a continuing basis. Projects are time-specific activities that create, enhance, or retire organizational resources or activities. So, programs are long-term ongoing activities, while projects are short-term efforts. The diagram on the next page shows how programs/projects should directly align with and map to strategic goal(s).

Enterprise Strategic Goals

Enterprise-Wide Strategic Initiatives

Line of Business #1 Goals	Line of Business #2 Goals	Line of Business #3 Goals
Line of Business #1 Program Group	Line of Business #2 Program Group	Line of Business #3 Program Group

Project 1-1	Project 1-2	Project 1-3	Project 2-1	Project 2-2	Project 2-3	Project 3-1	Project 3-2	Project 3-3

Capability Alignment

Resource Alignment

To further illustrate the goal-activity relationship, imagine that a $25 million anonymous donation is given to a new non-profit organization (NPO) that was founded to promote initiatives that clean-up pollution in current and former boatyard sites in Florida. Being new, the NPO only has general goals and has not yet established programs to address pollution at sites that the organization selects. There are several types of pollution on the grounds and dock area that violate State and Federal regulations, which are common to many current and former boatyards. The challenge for this NPO is to think along two tracks: (1) enduring goals, performance measures, and attainment programs; and (2) what is the best application of this initial large donation to support the establishment of effective ongoing programs that detect and remediate various forms of pollution, as well as an initial set of projects at high-priority sites to address specific pollutants. In that there are dozens of boatyard pollution types and remediation methods, the NPO likely does not have the resources or expertise to rapidly create remediation programs and targeted projects in all areas – so choices must be made on the mix of programs and projects – and that mix will likely change over time depending on internal and external stakeholder, regulatory, and technology factors.

An organization's future options are driven at both the strategic and tactical levels in three ways: new directions and goals; changing business priorities; and emerging technologies. The organizational architecture should not be altered unless there are changes to strategic direction and goals. These strategic changes are implemented when the line of business managers and their program managers provide the changes in business processes and priorities that are needed to accomplish the new goals. Also, the support/ delivery staff must identify viable enablers and technology solutions to support the new processes.

Another way to show how an organization thinks about itself and the accomplishment of important goals, is to use a "short story scenario" wherein some challenge is presented, and solutions are found - all told as a story. People like stories that have relevance and are interesting. An example is provided on the next two pages. Note that new capabilities are shown as planning assumptions, which are indicated as numbered side notes.

Making a Sale in 2023

Jeff Linder, Vice President of Industrial Sales for Garrett Manufacturing Company (GMC) had just finished a presentation at the 2023 National Highway Safety Conference along with Howard Garrett, GMC's CEO, who had teleconferenced in on the big display screen behind the podium.[1] As Jeff was leaving the main conference room, Andrea Newman, Director of Safety and Transportation for the State of Tennessee, asked Jeff if they could talk for a few minutes about the new line of solar-powered highway and street lights that GMC had just given a presentation on. [2, 3]

Planning Assumptions

1. New remote video teleconferencing capability.

2. Product roll-outs at National conferences.

3. Need to hold detailed product discussions on short notice, globally.

4. 24x7 work availability.

5. Increased suburban commuting and telecommuting.

6. Tracking of Government reports to anticipate product needs.

7. Changing population demographics, driving new product development.

"Thanks for taking a minute to talk Jeff. I want to tell you about a situation we have in Tennessee and see if your new product line can help" said Andrea as they found a table in the refreshment area.[4] "No problem, thanks for asking" Jeff said. Andrea pulled up a document on her tablet computer and said "Jeff, here is a report that shows an increasing number of serious accidents in rural areas of Tennessee involving passenger cars and agricultural equipment or commercial trucks. We've attributed it to the growth of suburban communities further out in the countryside that then depend on two-lane country roads for commuting into the city.[5] When you put slow tractors and trucks together with cars that are in a hurry at all hours to get somewhere, you have a recipe for disaster." "Isn't this problem being seen in other places around the country?" asked Jeff. "Yes, and one of the contributing factors that is consistently coming out of investigations of the night-time accidents is the lack of good lighting on these country roads.[6] I am thinking that your highway grade stand-alone solar light pole can help us provide more nighttime visibility on high-risk rural roads without having to invest in the supporting electrical infrastructure." [7, 8]

Jeff thought for a minute before responding. "You know, this new line of highway lights also has options to incorporate 911 emergency call boxes and Global Positioning System (GPS) equipment that can connect to both State and local level first responders.[9] This might be useful in also improving response times should an accident occur in spite of the improved lighting." Andrea nodded and said, "Yes, I doubt that better lighting will solve the entire problem, but it will help people see each other better, and these other options can improve accident response times, which will also save lives. What is the pricing like?"

8. Increased cost benefit of solar powered lights, which are eco-friendly.

9. Continued incorporation of additional product features to expand customer base.

10. Global use of smart phones for employee communication.

11. Integration of sales, marketing, and production information.

12. Accurate customer quotes on the fly.

Jeff pulled his smartphone[10] out of his pocket and connected to GMC's marketing and sales database at headquarters via a satellite Internet link.[11] "Andrea, these units are $11,300 each, including the GPS and 911 features." Andrea took notes and responded, "If I can get permission to conduct a pilot test in a couple of months can you provide the lights?" Jeff asked, "How many miles of road?" "About four miles in the particular area I'm thinking of," said Andrea. "Ok, the suggested density for the new unit is 18 per mile, so that would be 72 units total. I can give you our 10 percent early-adopter discount, so the total would be $732,240. Let me check what the shipping time would be." Jeff sent a high priority text to Bob Green, Vice President of Manufacturing. Bob was in the factory when he received Jeff's note on his phone, and after checking the GMC Production Scheduling System, he responded two minutes later that a special order for 72 units could be completed and shipped 35 days from when the order is received. Jim relayed this information to Andrea, who said, "Wow, that was fast. I have all the information I need to propose the pilot project. I'll get back to you in the next week."[12]

1.4 An Organization Has an Architecture

Basically, architecture looks at form and function. For holistic enterprise architecture (HEA), this includes the structure and socio/techno capabilities of all areas of a organization. I like to call this *"architecture for CEOs"* because no aspect is left out, which matches the scope of responsibilities of the top leader.

As with many aspects of an organization, there are formal and informal versions. The formal version tends to be driven by and adhere to documented policy, rules, and procedures. The informal versions are those with exist and are practiced but are not documented. Important elements are: who works for who, what information do I have access to, what location(s) do I work at, when do I take time off, and how am I evaluated?

It is important for an organization's leadership and enterprise architects to understand both the formal and informal sources of power and decision-making, which underpin how, where, when, and by whom work is done. In that people have free will and agreement on decisions is often not universal, it is normal for a socio/techno organization to have dissention and divergence in rule making and rule following activities. The informal activities can have a positive, balancing effect if they reflect differences in a productive, professional manner. The informal activities become unhelpful and toxic if they are expressed in obstructive, harmful ways – unless – they are countering harmful, unfair, and perhaps illegal formal policies and functions – which unfortunately does occur. In that case, one hopes that notification is made to appropriate authorities.

The much more normal situation is that there is a mix of documented official policy/methods along with unofficial ways of doing things. In any case, the enterprise architecture should be an accurate reflection of structure and function. An effective holistic approach to enterprise architecture is one that it is able to be used with organizations in any area of the public, private, and non-profit sectors. While each sector imposes some differences, these are usually minor in comparison to the similarities of how an organization is structured and operated. Hospitals, universities, agencies, and businesses all over the world have far more in common with their sector peers then have differences.

In documenting structure and function, a holistic enterprise architecture must be able to scale between high, mid, and low-level views in a consistent manner. This produces traceable inter-dependencies and exposes capability gaps and overlaps.

The holistic, scalable enterprise architecture gets its value through its completeness, accuracy, and acceptance among leadership and business units. This occurs only when there is strong ongoing CEO support, matched by support by the other executives, senior managers, and staff. That support will not be found if there is a reluctance to have structure and functions properly and openly documented. Unfortunately, support for enterprise architecture is often not found for a variety of reasons: none of which have merit. Hidden agendas, a lack of awareness of holistic methods, inter-personal conflicts, competition for limited resources, and perceptions of unfair treatment by employees can lead to a lack of support for the development and support of a single authoritative baseline reference on structure and functions.

Regardless of whether an organization decides to document itself through a formalized holistic architecture, the following basic relationships will be present: the mission purpose is the context for setting strategic goals (S), which *drive* business/data (B) functions, that are *enabled* by various types of technology (T) systems and host networks/infrastructure.

Bottom line: Each organization has a structure and a set of functions at many levels, so it has an enterprise architecture. The question is whether this enterprise architecture is formally recognized, documented, and used to support planning and decision-making. If not, the architecture exists informally in pockets, and the focus is on specific solutioning.

The practice of holistic enterprise architecture (HEA) is unique in its ability to develop an integrated set of scalable views that can be understood by executives, managers, and technical experts. By using the same HEA framework, organizations with different structures and functions can be compared, which supports restructuring decision making.

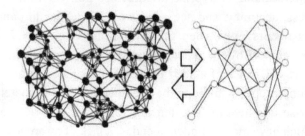

The underlying analytic model that HEA uses is the "Cube" framework, which includes aspect views for structure, function, services, valuation, risk, and culture – as well as sub-architecture domains for strategy, business, data, systems, infrastructure, security, skills, and standards. This framework can be used to model any type of organization, regardless of sector (e.g., public, private, or non-profit).

As mentioned, the Cube Framework's six faces provide organizing relationships and touchpoints for the fundamental aspects of any organization: structure, function, services, risk, assets, and culture. This is depicted in the following two views of the cube: top/front and bottom/back (since only three sides of a cube are visible at a time). More detailed descriptions of the framework and each face are provided in Appendix B.

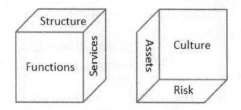

A more applied depiction of how the framework covers the basic elements of an organization is shown in the following figure, wherein the framework is presented as an office building with floors and towers that represent the architectural domains and threads.

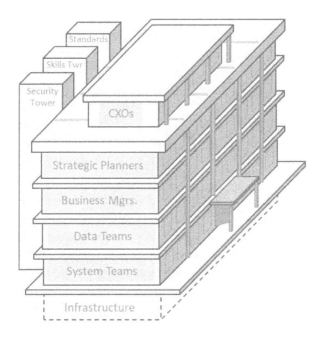

On the side face, the five major sub-architecture "domains" are shown hierarchically, in that strategic goals drive business workflows/dataflows that have manual and digitized elements, supported by systems that are hosted on networks in buildings. The three vertical sub-architecture "threads" are represented as vertical towers that have touchpoints to each of the domains. For example, many types of security and privacy controls exist, which relate to the business, data, and system domains within and between business units.

In another example, the skills that are required for organizational strategic planners are different from those of business managers and analysts, which are different from data and system administrators, application programmers, or network engineers. All of these controls and skills are needed in organizations that provide products and services in today's digitized global operating environment.

Section 2

Pre-Deal / Two Organizations

2.1 Why Mergers & Acquisitions Occur

2.2 Architecture in Positioning to Sell

2.3 Architecture in Acquisitions

2.4 Architecture in Mergers

2.5 Architecture During Deal-Making

Section 2

Pre-Deal / Separate Organizations

2.1 Why Mergers & Acquisitions Occur

An organization is created for reason(s) that relate to the wants and needs of the founders as well as the opportunities and threats that exist in the environment at the time. Over time, the founders change so the wants and needs of top decision-makers change, and on a parallel track, the environmental opportunities/threats change as well. As such, reasons for organizational existence and ownership change, sometimes to an extent that the best path forward is to buy, sell, or merge part or all of an organization. The following are examples of why owners or stewards (e.g., Boards, estate executors) decide to buy, sell, or merge an organization:[7]

Buying:
- o   Acquire intellectual property
- o   Expand customer base
- o   Lower transactional costs
- o   Diversify investment portfolio
- o   Desire to be part of something new

Selling:
- o   Recover equity
- o   Death of founder
- o   Low/no profitability
- o   Legal mandate
- o   New leader vision

Merging:
- o   Increase market share
- o   Address competitive pressures
- o   Cost/revenue/resource synergies
- o   Economies of scale
- o   Managerial self-interest

---

[7] Organizational creation (start-up) is not part of this discussion, as it involves specific and unique drivers, resources, and legalities. See Section 4.4 for details.

Buying, selling, or merging an organization are distinctly different endeavours. Additionally, each organization is a unique socio-techno-legal entity that has attributes which determine whether an approach will or won't be effective in post-deal restructuring. This includes culture, processes, skill-base, assets, liquidity, and law/regulatory requirements.

The following sections discuss how holistic enterprise architecture methods can make valuable contributions to an organization that is preparing itself to be sold or is evaluating other candidate organizations to buy or to merge with.

2.2 Architecture in Positioning to Sell

There are several reasons for an owner (or stewards) to decide to sell the organization, including wanting to cash-out, inheritors don't want to run the organization, or preserving legacy by placing the organization with a more capable owner.

Regardless of the reason to sell, for the organization to fetch a top price or find the best legacy steward, there has to be a clear, comprehensive understanding of structure, functions, resources, culture, and legal obligations… as well as a way to share that with prospective buyers.

As mentioned in Chapter 2, Holistic Enterprise Architecture (HEA) is unique in its ability to create a range of management-friendly and technically detailed views of all or parts of an organization. Accordingly, HEA can be helpful to organizations that want to be able to present themselves to potential buyers with clarity and consistency.

An experienced, independent HEA consultant should be hired, and an internal executive-level facilitator should be named. The two foundational models that should then be created are the enterprise's cube framework and an overview diagram.

The HEA Framework can initially be populated with information from the strategic plan, organization chart, service catalog, general ledger, employee roster, and asset inventories for data, systems, facilities, and capital equipment. Some or all of these documents may be out of date or not exist, in which case the internal lead executive should set up interview sessions with the appropriate executives, managers, and staff who can provide this information. These sessions can be conducted onsite or online, with a space assigned to this project that can accommodate up to a dozen people and support computer presentations with large screens and the review of reports and large-scale drawings. Access to the organization's files and the ability to create scalable electronic and printed documents and diagrams are also needed.

For example, at Danbridge Health, the organization is composed of a headquarters office, three hospitals, six walk-in clinics, a medical transport service, and a medical supplies warehouse. An updated 5-Year Strategic Plan was published that identifies goals, strategic initiatives, and roles for specific executives and program or facility directors. As such, the basic DH Enterprise Framework will look like this (to the right):

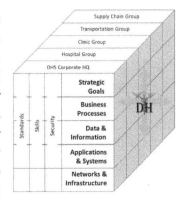

Complimenting the framework is the overview diagram, which shows structure, functions, and assets that are organized as a matrix (the columns are the business units, and the rows are the sub-architecture domains).[8]

---

[8] The author gratefully acknowledges the influence and mentoring of two of the developers of the foundational concepts and methods of enterprise architecture – John Zachman and Stephen Spewak. See Appendix B for details.

	Business Unit 1	Business Unit 2	Business Unit 3	Business Unit 4
Goals Domain				
Process Domain				
Data Domain				
Systems Domain				
Infra. Domain				

This documentation should be maintained as a printable electronic diagram on a secure internal computer system, wherein the images are clickable to navigate to more detailed views and information/images about goals, processes, data collections, systems, and capital assets. A discussion of related artifacts is presented in Section 4.3.[9]

Here are types of documentation for each Framework area:

Strategic Domain: Founding Request/Approvals/Charter, Strategic Plan/Goal Tracker, Mission/Vision Statements, Incorporation Docs, SEC/IRS Requests/Approvals, SWOT Analyses, Balanced Scorecards, External Enterprise Assessments, Government Regulations, Legal Filings/Decisions, Organization Chart, Board of Directors Policies.

---

[9] Other architecture approaches exist that have areas of strength in their application but are not holistic in scope, covering all aspects of an organization. Examples are the DODAF Framework that is good for systems architecture, as well as TOGAF which is good for specific solutioning work. Either can be used as a best practice method in the systems, data, or business domains of the Cube Framework.

Business Domain: Business Plans, Annual/Quarterly Reports, Financials Summary/General Ledger, Local Strategic Plans/Goals, Services Catalog, Workflow Diagrams, Process Models, Work Breakdown Structures, Role/Responsibility Matrices, Use Cases, Program/Project Plans, Supply Chain Plans/Results. Asset Lists.

Data Domain: Knowledge Management Plan, Enterprise Data Plan and Inventory, Master Data Management Plan, Object Diagrams, Entity Relationship Diagrams, Dataflow Diagrams, Object Library, Data Dictionary, Data Policies, Knowledge Transfer Plan.

Systems Domain: Systems Inventory, Software Catalog, Systems Interface Diagrams, Systems Overview Diagrams, Technology Roadmaps, Designs, Lifecycle Development Policy, Project Plans, Rack Elevation Diagrams, Network Engineering Diagrams, Network Operations Center Policies and Procedures. Disaster Recovery Docs.

Infrastructure Domain: Building Blueprints, Cable Plant Diagrams, Utility Diagrams/Specs, Data/Server Room Diagrams, Equipment Lists, Environmental Regulations/Compliance Docs, Campus Plans.

Security Thread: Risk Management Plan, Security Plan, Data Privacy Plan, Security Controls List, Authority to Operate Docs, Security Audits, Security Operations Center Policies and Procedures.

Skills Thread: HR Overviews and Policies, Compensation Plan, Payroll Summaries, Pension Plan Summaries, Skill/Training Plans.

Standards Thread: Standards Lists and Policies, Configuration Management Docs, Reference Architectures, SOPs.

Some of this documentation exists and can be harvested, some does not exist and will have to be developed. The documentation that exists is often not in the format or degree of completeness that the HEA approach calls for, so the HEA team needs to do interpretation and drill-down/gap filling.

As in selling a house, if I were the owner or CEO of an organization that was to be put on the market for sale, I would put top priority on "getting the house in order" and ready to be presented to potential buyers.

Home buyers are looking at location, curb appeal, size, flow, condition, and documented compliance with building codes. These are common sense items - no reasonable buyer would want to buy a house that is in bad shape, out of compliance, or burned down unless they plan to do a major remodel or tear it down and put up something else. In those cases, the buyer wants a significant discount from the price that top-condition comparable homes are being sold for, or they may only be willing to pay for the land.

In looking to sell a company, there are a number of similarities that should be paid attention to, including audience, market conditions, the value of assets individually and collectively, legal entanglements, and degree of motivation to do a deal.

The Holistic Enterprise Architecture practices that are presented in this book can help to get an organization ready to be sold, transferred, restructured, or disestablished. For HEA to be effective, there has to be CEO and management support.

Without this, HEA assessment, documentation and presentation activities will be incomplete, inconsistent, and drawn-out. None of that is helpful to the organization and is a reflection of a lack of leadership effectiveness, business unit inefficiencies, and cultural disfunction. Unfortunately, this bad situation is found all too frequently in organizations or all types and sizes – with a pending sale, hostile takeover, or legal restructuring directive being the only way to move them forward and serving to spotlight those problems.

So, is a problem-ridden organization beyond being able to be helped by HEA to get itself in order and improve its value? No, not if the CEO is championing the effort and making it an all-hands project with top priority.

For organizations that are well led, effectively run, and formally documented, the HEA project can serve as a new best practice that helps to organize, align, resolve gaps/overlaps, and explain in plain language the evidence (artifacts) that will be used to present the organization to prospective buyers.

Will organizational assets be sold together or in pieces? Unless there is a legal requirement or the express desire of current ownership, both options should be assessed and incorporated into sales presentations. An example of the assets of the case study organization is presented as follows:

Hospital #1	Clinic A	Clinic D	HQ Office
Hospital #2	Clinic B	Clinic E	Transport Svc.
Hospital #3	Clinic C	Clinic F	Supply Center
Customer Data	Cash/Debt		Patents/Other IP

Do the HEA activities have to take weeks, months, or years to complete? Not necessarily, but again, it depends on CEO and all-hands support and participation. An experienced HEA practitioner with access to the CEO and all employees on a priority basis can create the framework and overview diagram in a day, but drill-down details will be limited to links to documentation that already exists. Still, the framework and overview are uniquely helpful in depicting the scope and functions of the organization… and further analyses and documentation work can be added to these foundational models. HEA documents should be kept in a secure online repository and with limited access along with printed copies.

The following provides the amount of HEA documentation that can be accomplished in several timeframes:

Time	Scope	Purpose	Deliverables
1 day	Whole Organization	Overview	FW, OD, OC, GLS
1 week	Whole + BUs	BU Capabilities	+ BU Overviews
1 mo.	Whole + BUs + Domains	Process, Asset Overview	+ Domain Models
6 mo.	Detailed Whole, Bus + Domains	Process, Asset Details	All
2 yrs.	Detailed Whole, Bus + Domains	Cultural Incorporation	All + Annual Updates

FW=Framework, OD=Overview Diagram, OC=Org. Chart, GLS=General Ledger Summary, BU=Business Unit, DO=Data Overview, SNO=Systems/Nets Overview, WM=Workflow Models, DM=Data Models, SM=System Models, SC=Security Controls

The result should be that the organization can be more clearly presented to potential buyers, with artifact evidence that will support seller claims on the value, condition, conformance, and flexibility of the entire company and/or its parts. Clearly and consistently showing the organization in total and in parts, is how HEA helps a seller to get the top possible price.

The following is a rough cost estimate to develop a HEA:

Project Timeframe	Senior-Level HEA Architect ($150/hr)	Mid-Level HEA Architect ($120/hr)	HEA Modeler ($90/hr)	Total Est. Cost
1-day	1 x 8hrs	0	0	$1,200
1-week	2 x 40hrs	0	1 x 40hrs	$15,600
1-month	2 x 160hrs	0	1 x 160hrs	$62,400
6-months	2 x 160hrs x 6mo.	2 x 160hrs x 6 mo.	2 x 160hrs x 6mo	$691,200
2-years	2 x 160hrs x 24mo	2 x 160hrs x 24mo	2 x 160hrs x 24mo	$2,764,800

HEA User Training Workshop (1-Day) = $3,000

Again, it is in a selling organization's best interest to be able to present itself well to prospective buyers. Adopting HEA is part of that, but having the right "selling prep team" is essential too. The following are the positions and roles that are recommended for the selling prep team (* are external experts).

Position	Role
Owner(s)	Approve approach, sign deal
Board Members	Receive briefings, give advice
CEO	Approve approach, lead negotiations
Chief Counsel	Ensure legalities, advise owners
COO	Lead briefer, assess sale offers/risk

CFO	Present financials, assess sale offers
CTO	Present/assess tech capabilities/risks
CHCO	Present/assess staff/culture issues
Chief Architect	Ensure structure/functions documented
Staff Analysts	Support analyses, modelling, briefings
Risk Analyst	Identify threats/mitigation options
Briefer	Coordinate internal/external comms
M&A Broker*	Develop approach, attract buyers
M&A Counsel*	Advise on M&A law and offers
M&A Banker*	Represent bank, advise on financials
HEA Architect*	Advise on enterprise structure issues
M&A Analysts*	Perform scenario/financial assessments

There are many reasons for wanting to sell an organization and many reasons for wanting to buy, which makes for many possible scenarios. Some scenarios involve personal and professional hostility and intrigue, others are transparent and calm. Some scenarios drag out for months/years, others run fast in days/weeks. Some are free of legal entanglements, others attract litigation and/or require government approval.

Regardless, it is the only the owners and/or stewards who can sign a deal once the legalities are satisfied. The purpose of the selling prep team is to ensure that the organization is effectively documented, valued, and presented; that potential buyers are aware of the offering and can perform due diligence; that purchase scenarios are identified and analysed; that legalities are addressed; and that a deal is made ready.

The selling prep team should be provided with a private and securable working space, such as a conference room in an access-controlled area. This room should be reserved for the team's use for the duration of the M&A activities, which could last several or many months. Door cipher locks and window blinds should be installed to ensure privacy. A stand-alone private computer network should be installed, with no connection to other internal/external networks. Desktop PCs, a server, several conferencing phones, printer/copier, displays, and videoconferencing equipment should be provided. A clearly marked single desktop PC and cabled connection should be available in the room for internet queries. A rack of lockboxes outside the room should be provided for team members to store their phones and laptops while in the team room. No removable media (e.g., USB drives, external hard drives) or recording devices should be allowed in the room. The security concepts and rules for the room should be briefed and acknowledged in writing, along with a signed Non-Disclosure Agreement (NDA) by each member.

Existing electronic and hardcopy internal documentation on the organizational should be gathered and organized for the team by the Briefer, with assistance from the other team members as may be necessary. Having a complete set of financial, HR, legal, operational, technology, and infrastructure documentation is essential to developing an accurate and complete set of overviews and detailed summaries of the organizations structure, functions, and assets – all of which contribute to developing the initial valuation figure – what the organization is worth. Additional analyses may be needed to examine the viability and valuation of if specific parts of the organization were to be sold separately, and what the value of the remaining organization would then be. These analyses will determine what a defendable sales price should be.

Estimating the value of an organization is not only dependent on the quality and completeness of supporting documentation, but also on industry "rules-of-thumb" for financials and operations, as well as regulations/approvals, legal actions, unique intellectual property, capital assets, brand strength, technology utilization/currency, and intangibles such as customer loyalty.

The following is an example of a rough estimation of the value of the case study private organization (DH):

Type		(Annual $000)	Notes (Annual average over 3 years)
Assets	Cash/CDs	7,860	On Deposit
	Accts. Recv	42,359	Patient + Services Billing
	Capital Eq	12,682	5-Yr Depreciation Schedule
	R&D Grants	1,431	Govt & Private Grants (7)
	Patents	1,203	10-Yr Effective Period
		65,535	

	Accts. Pay	9,665	Supplies, External Services
	Salary/Bon.	38,108	Yr Total for all Employees (359)
	Pensions	2,580	Yr Total for Vested Employees (43)
Liabilities	Owner Profit	3,100	Average Annual Cash Payment
	Loan	3,086	General Ops / 3-Yr Loan Period
	Capital Eq.	8,252	3-Year Purchase Period
	Legal Special	744	Settlement of Legal Cases (3)
		65,535	
Annual Profit x 5 Yrs.		15,500	Projected Earning Potential
Other Assets – Current Value		23,176	Current Liquidatable Assets
Brand Recognition/Loyalty		5,000	Preference for DH Services
Overall Valuation		**43,253**	*Verified by XYZ CPA Firm on 3/4/24*

Please note that this is a simplified example of a privately held company with no shareholders or complex investments. That said, hopefully you can see that there are various types of assets and liabilities, many of which have specific rules for depreciation, averaging, payment, etc. It is the net total of these assets and liabilities, extrapolated out for several years, along with special market factor that all add up to a defendable market valuation. Whether a buyer is willing to pay the $43 million valuation price is dependent on degree of motivation, clarity of analysis, and support of stakeholders.

HEA helps create clarity and completeness in analyses, which builds both buyer and seller confidence, as well as reducing the prospect of post-deal surprises or legal entanglements.

2.3 Architecture in Buying an Organization

There are many reasons for one organization to want to buy another organization.[10] Reasons include increasing market share, decreasing competition, adding products or services, ownership of patented products or processes, brand strengthening, access to current and potential customer data, acquiring debt to offset high profits, management's egos, harness excess capacity, gain access to special expertise, increase manufacturing

---

[10] Additional options are a merger or hostile takeover, which are covered in Section 2.4.

capability, improve supply chains, and diversify the product and service portfolio.

Whatever the buyer's reasons are, there needs to be a clear understanding of the objectives, the measurements of success, and the method to thoroughly and accurately evaluate candidate organization(s) that might be purchased – doing so before negotiations on price and terms begin. Examples of measurable goals for purchasing are as follows:

- Increase market share by > 12% over the prior year (PY).
- Obtain 3 new patented processes for making X & Y.
- Diversify by adding 4 new product lines.
- Increase supply chain output by > 9% over PY.
- Increase brand recognition (Q) > 10% over PY.
- Gain 2 experienced eCommerce channel sales teams.
- Lower materials cost for X & Y by > 6% over PY.
- Increase D & E group product orders by > 8% over PY.

When actively tracked, these measures of success can provide near-term and long-term post-deal feedback in assessing whether the acquisition was worth doing – whether the most important objectives were met (was it a success). It should be acknowledged that in the months/years after an acquisition, market conditions will change, new products and methods are introduced by competitors, consumer preferences change, and new government standards or regulations may be introduced. But even with those changes, the attainment of identified primary goals for the merger should be determined and factored into future planning for the merged organization.

There are plenty of studies, stories, and antidotes about unsuccessful corporate acquisitions,[11][12] with the primary problem being an inability to

---

[11] McKinsey & Co. (August 2019). Done deal? Why many large transactions fail to cross the finish line? *"Our research shows that many large mergers and acquisitions are abandoned before closing because of value-creation, regulatory, and political issues."*
[12] Harvard Business Review (March 2020). Don't Make this Common M&A Mistake. *"According to most studies, between 70 and 90 percent of acquisitions fail. Explanations for this depressing number emphasize problems with integrating the two parties involved… executives can dramatically increase their odds of success if they understand how to select targets, how much to pay for them, and whether and how to integrate them."*

blend the two separate organizations into one effective organization. Not all of the parts of each organization are retained, especially those that are duplicated. But even with the major gaps and overlaps being identified, there is ineffective action in creating a well-functioning whole. A big part of the problem is dissimilar views, as they use different business/ technology frameworks.

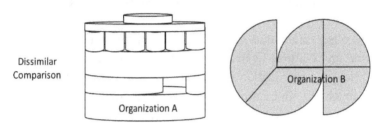

This is where HEA can help. Using the same holistic framework to model both organizations allows for likewise comparison and better identification of extraneous elements.

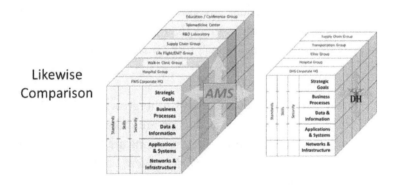

An M&A "acquisition team" composition is similar to that of a M&A selling prep team (described earlier), with the exception of adding more people who specialize in finding target organizations whose capabilities and characteristics will meet the primary objectives for doing the acquisition.

Each candidate organization needs to be vetted in terms of important tangible items (e.g., structure, functions, financials, market share, competitive strategy, assets, legal issues) as well as intangible items (e.g., cultural fit, knowledge transfer, customer loyalty). This type of vetting requires likewise comparative analyses, with an eye toward meeting a particular objective and/or identifying potential obstacles in post-deal restructuring. Sometimes, it is best to keep all or parts of an acquired organization in their own semi-independent operating sphere until assets, customers, staff, systems, and processes can be more easily and effectively migrated into the buying organization. In other cases, the acquired organization is never assimilated, but run as a subordinate independent business unit.

It is my observation that many M&A deals are done in spite of poor structural and cultural fit between the buying and selling organizations. Sometimes, an organization is bought for certain assets that are deemed to have unusually high current or future value. Sometimes a deal is done as part of a leadership initiative to show growth, keep competitors from gaining an advantage, or maintain activities that may be seen as sector leadership – even if the fit or numbers are not optimal. Egotistical or myopic executives might say "just do the deal!"

As was mentioned before, research by *Harvard Business Review* and other reputable research organizations has shown that the failure rate for mergers and acquisitions is quite high…. more than two-thirds.[13] So why do M&A deals keep happening in the numbers that we see? I would point to several factors:

- Management bonuses are often tied to growth.
- Perceptions of visionary leadership are linked with growth.
- Legal, banking, consulting commissions are high ($ millions).
- Departure "golden parachutes" for executives are high.
- Gives gratification to egotistical executives.
- Prevents competitors from gaining an advantage.
- Stock prices can increase, along with shareholder support.
- Accountability for failure is delayed and/or negligible.
- Breakup value can exceed the purchase price.
- Payment can be in many forms (cash, stock, assets, IP, barter).
- Government regulations change.

As such, I believe that M&A acquisitions will continue to be robust in most market conditions. The motivations may shift in bull markets and

---

[13] Harvard Business Review (March 2020). Don't Make this Common M&A Mistake.

bear markets.... from good values, to low purchase prices, to wanting to block competitors, to having a change in leadership, to regulatory changes. Opportunities abound, but the real challenge is in avoiding toxic purchases and being effective in managing post-deal restructuring activities, unless parallel/separated operations are planned.

2.4 Architecture in a Merger of Peers

The term "mergers", as used in this book, indicates a situation where two organizations are coming together as equals (peers). There is no superior or subordinate, which often complicates the post-deal restructuring process. Parts or all of both organizations may survive with their original name and brands, some mixing and sunsetting may occur, or a single new organization is formed with a new name and portfolio of old and new products and services. In a merger of peers, several issues must be decided prior to the deal being signed:

- The structure and roles of the executive team.
- Compensation for departing executives and managers.
- The name and branding of the new organization.
- Ownership and treatment of former names and brands.
- Consolidation of all financials.
- Pending legal issues, past decisions/awards.
- Consolidation of all HR functions, records, and positions.
- Consolidation of workflows, selection of best methods.
- Consolidation of asset, data, IP, inventories.
- Designation and operation of autonomous units.
- Board of Directors consolidation, changes, composition.
- Public communications, government liaison.
- Continuation/termination of outside partnerships.
- Management and staff compensation policies.
- Governance groups for enterprise-wide operations.

Cultural differences between the peers must also be identified and dealt with as a priority. Clashes of cultures and/or disenfranchisement of groups is a major cause of failed mergers. Creating a healthy, inclusive environment is paramount. HEA can support change management and building a new culture by providing views of the old and new organizations in all dimensions.

2.5 Architecture During Deal-Making

The deal-making phase of M&A activities is when the selling team, the buying team and their brokers, bankers, lawyers, and advisors meet in closed sessions to discuss, negotiate, and hopefully agree to the terms of sale of an organization to another organization or the merger of two peers. Sometimes the terms of the sale or merger must be approved by a Board of Directors, shareholder groups, and/or government agencies. Once the terms are agreed to and the sale or merger documents are signed, then the deal-making phase ends and the post-deal restructuring begins on the designated effective date. The new owners take over, or in a merger of equals, the new blended executive team begins in their designated roles.

As with many legal proceedings, applicable laws and regulations must be adhered to and confidentiality is enforced through Non-Disclosure Agreements (that should be put in place during the pre-deal due diligence phase).

Attendees at deal-making sessions have historically centered on legal and financial experts, but due to the increased role that technology plays, experts in enterprise-wide and focused technologies are being added to the teams. These experts need to be readily available to the principal deal makers. Experienced Holistic Enterprise Architects can advise on business alignment, portfolio blending, and overall technology fit as they identify the strong and weak aspects of the selling or merging organizations. This may affect the price that the buyer is willing to pay, unless the seller can explain and perhaps demonstrate how an area of concern – hence risk – can be or will be mitigated (taken care of).

Bottom line: much of the value of HEA analyses is seen during pre-deal due diligence and post-deal restructuring. These HEA analyses can also be valuable during the deal's actual negotiations and these holistic architects should be available.

Section 3

Post-Deal / One Organization

3.1 Form Follows Function

3.2 Likewise Comparison

3.3 Coming Together

3.4 Moving Forward

Section 3

Post-Deal / One Organization

3.1 Form Follows Function[14]

In an ideal world, how an organization is structured will reflect the purposes it serves, with no waste from non-aligned activities. In the real world, many organizations are spin-offs, modifications, or fusions of other prior organizations; with each original strand having a different purpose, history, culture, and track record. As such, an organization often has a mix of cultures and programs from the past that are not fully oriented with current goals and methods.

This heterogenous, non-optimized condition can be found in many organizations. This is then made worse by continuing to engage in M&A activities and onboard all or part of other formerly independent organizations, without effective alignment and restructuring. Holistic EA is really the only way that an organization's leadership can develop and maintain a useful overview of the changing organization that supports planning and decision-making.

The goal of HEA is to provide a complete and accurate set of views and supporting documentation for the enterprise and its parts, to whatever level of detail is needed for current operations and future planning. This includes being able to see the reporting structure, the intra- and inter-program workflows and dataflows, the enabling systems and infrastructure. The rest of this Section provides examples of the documentation that is most helpful.

---

[14] The phrase "form follows function" is attributed to architect Louis H. Sullivan in his 1896 essay "The Tall Office Building Artistically Considered" whereby a skyscraper's exterior design should reflect the different interior functions. Famous architect Frank Lloyd Wright later said that this phase has been misunderstood… "form and function should be one, joined in a spiritual union."

3.2 Likewise Comparison

The post-deal goal is to bring two organizations together and form a new single well-functioning organization that can successfully compete. Sometimes the post-deal plan is to let the acquired organization continue to operate independently, but that is not a good long-term approach due to duplicated overhead costs. A likewise comparison is essential either way.

This likewise comparison should be scalable and management friendly (clear with no jargon). It is best done using the same holistic framework (e.g., the Cube) and includes an overview model and more detailed process, system, and data models.

I have found that there is lots of variation in the types of enterprise-wide and sub-component models that I have seen over my 45+ years of working with business, government, military, and academic organizations. This variation made it difficult to compare the capabilities of two organizations, so I took the best aspects of several business and technology architecture approaches and created a higher-level holistic framework that correlates the elements. The Cube Framework (below) can be used with any type of organization.

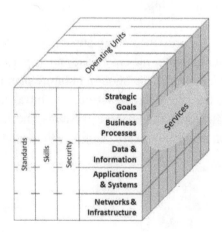

This is an example of using the Cube Framework to compare the two heath care organizations in the case study (Section 4):

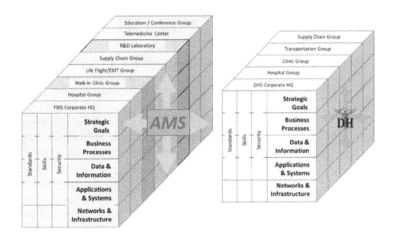

Each slice (segment) of the overall cube represents a sub-unit in the organization that contains unique capabilities and services (verticals) and subscribes to enterprise-wide services (crosscuts). In modelling each segment on its own, all of the sub-architecture levels of the front face of the cube are retained, while the top face reflects more granular sub-units in that segment (e.g., program offices), and the side face again reflects the unique vertical and cross-cutting enterprise services that the segment provides and consumes as part of the overall organization. Here are the "cubes within cubes":

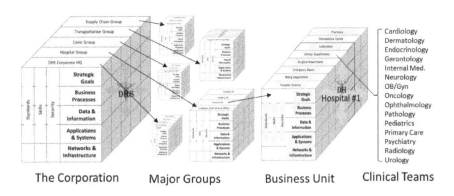

Scaling the architecture in a consistent way is achieved through this type of decomposition and aggregation. You can say that there are "cubes, within cubes, within cubes" as a reminder that consistent scaling preserves the content and purpose of each of the cubes faces. The most important of these are: (1) the top face, which shows structure as derived from the organization chart, and (2) the front face, which hierarchically shows the sub-architecture domains.

After establishing the cube, developing an overview diagram is the next step in doing a likewise architectural comparison:

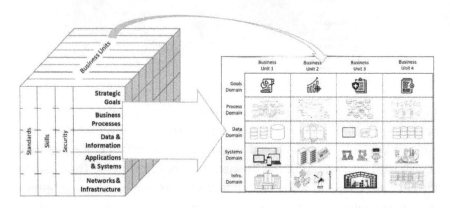

The overview diagram uses icons at each domain level to indicate the presence of a workflow, a data collection, a system, or an infrastructure item. The electronic version of the diagram allows a user to click on any icon to get to a more detailed model. These models include flowcharts, interface diagrams, use cases, inventories, network engineering diagrams, various types of reports, and specification sheets. The models should be prepared using standard notations and formats to promote widespread adoption and easier analysis. Examples include Business Process Modeling Notation, Unified Modeling Language, Object-Oriented Design and Analysis. Reference Architectures refer to standardized, reusable designs that vendor products will work well with. The following is an example of a populated overview diagram.

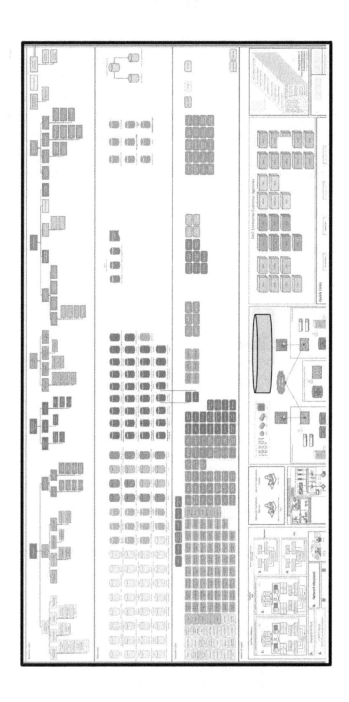

3.3 Coming Together (Restructuring)

Once the M&A deal is signed, unless government approval is required, the buying and selling organizations can begin to come together. It is important that the buying organization has a game plan for organizing and executing the merging of the two organizations, or the policies and procedures for the acquired organization to operate semi-independently. The quicker that key decisions and integration actions can be executed, the better.... as employees don't respond well to "in limbo" situations. That said, speed should not preclude discussion of challenges and opportunities all along the way. Agile methods and short sprints are a good best practice to use. The following is an outline of restructuring topics:

1. **Initial Set-up**
   a. Designate the Chief Restructuring Executive (CRE)
   b. Designate/Set-up a Dedicated Team Area
   c. Identify Restructuring Team & Managers (RTMs)

2. **Rules of the Road**
   a. Review Merger Deal & Legal Regulations
   b. Guidance from CEO, Stakeholder Considerations

3. **Envisioning the New Organization**
   a. Develop Restructuring Guiding Principles
   b. Identify Business Needs & Goals
   c. Develop List of Challenges & Opportunities
   d. Develop Initial Enterprise Architecture Design
   e. Create a Prioritized Actions List
   f. Create an Implementation Schedule & Tracker
   g. Create an Access-Controlled Documentation Library

4. **Restructuring Activities**
   a. Create Targeted Working Groups
   b. Start Regular Internal/External Briefings
   c. Set-up Employee Assistance Desk
   d. Hold Daily Team Meetings
   e. Track Progress & Remove Obstacles
   f. Identify Restructuring End, Do Lessons Learned

Phase 1. Initial Set-Up

1a. Designate the Chief Restructuring Executive (CRE).

While the acquiring (or lead) organization's CEO is ultimately responsible for all aspects of the M&A deal and it's the restructuring results that count the most.... whether a mission-effective and cost-efficient new organization created. That CEO has many ongoing responsibilities, yet the onboarding of a new organization and related restructuring decisions and actions require a top-level executive who is dedicated to this task. I suggest that this executive be at the same level as those CXOs just below the CEO, and be designated as the "Chief Restructuring Executive" (CRE) with a time-limited set of duties. The CRE should be introduced by the CEO who provides strong support throughout the restructuring process. The CEO should chair an Executive Steering Committee, CRE leads the Restructuring Mgmt. Team, the Restructuring Project Manager (PM) leads Work Groups.

1b. Designate/Set-up a Dedicated Team Area.

The Restructuring Team will need a dedicated, access-controlled space to be able to hold meetings, discuss sensitive issues, make decisions, and review documentation. Ideally, the area will be near the CEO and CXO areas to make their participation in meetings easier and to project the image of top-level support. The area should be connected to the organization's communications and computing networks, but should also have a stand-alone information network that allows for secure storage and retrievable of sensitive and in-work documentation, assessments, and decisions. It is important to remember that the organization's finances, operational capabilities, and employee careers are involved, which required special handling and protection.

1c. Identify Restructuring Teams & Managers (RTMs).

The CRE should work with the CEO and CXOs to identify the organizational members who will be assigned to the restructuring team, full-time at first, and then part-time until actions in their area are sufficiently completed. The following are recommended teams and skill areas:

Executive Steering Committee (ESC)
- o CEO (Chair), CXOs, CRE, Board Representative
- o Select Former CXOs – acquired organization
- o Restructuring PM & Secretary

Restructuring Management Team (RMT)
- o CRE (Chair)
- o Senior Directors/Managers
- o Select Management – acquired organization
- o Restructuring PM & Secretary

Focused Working Groups (WGs)
- o Working Group Leader (a RMT member)
- o Relevant Business Unit Manager(s)
- o Subject Matter Experts
- o Analysts and a Recorder

Restructuring decisions and implementation actions need to move rapidly whenever possible. An organization in limbo is an organization adrift, not able to fully or effectively address risks and opportunities presented by changes in the operating environment, new regulations, and competitor actions.

Some decisions are made as part of deal negotiations, so those actions may be more rapidly implemented, such as governance and major business unit adjustments. Supporting actions that relate new roles and resources will take longer if integration or retirement are the objective. This includes workflows, data collections, systems, networks, and facilities.

Phase 2. Rules of the Road

2a. Review Merger Deal & Legal Regulations.

The M&A "deal" is a legal agreement to bring two organizations together. The agreement must be consistent with law, stipulate types/amounts/methods/timeframes for payment, and designate key leadership positions and incumbents (which may include some executives from the acquired organization). This particularly true in the merger of equals where leaders from both organizations are identified to form a new combined leadership team. It is important that the Restructuring Management Team be familiar with the legal requirements and provisions of the deal. These should be reviewed by the ESC and RMT as a first order of business.

2b. Guidance from CEO, Stakeholder Considerations.

Beyond the legal and regulatory requirements, the ESC and RMT must understand the guiding principles and primary objectives of the newly combined organization, including viewpoints of the CEO and the interests of key stakeholders (e.g., business unit leaders, union leaders, strategic external partners, customer groups). To maintain consistency and unity in the restructuring effort, the CEO's guidance and approach must be followed by the CRE and in all RMT and WG implementation actions. The CEO's guidance may include overall business performance objectives, major structural changes, parallel operation instructions/timeframes, conflict resolution method, and the primary concerns of stakeholders.

Phase 3. Envisioning the New Organization.

Keeping the legal mandates and CEO guidance in mind, the CRE and Chief Enterprise Architect should begin discussions with the ESC and RMT on the new combined organization.

3a. Develop Guiding Principles.

There are several approaches to combining two organizations:

- Eliminate the selling organization
- Eliminate the buying organization
- Combine the best elements of each organization
- Operate the two organizations independently
- Adopt a totally new organizational structure

The approach is often decided by the CEO with advice from the Board and major stakeholders. If not, the CRE, CEA, and RMT members should prepare a briefing, with assistance from the Restructuring Team, on the pros and cons of each approach for CEO/Board decision. Once decided, the most important guiding principles need to be developed with the CEO and ESC:

- Targets for workforce size and operating locations
- Cultural considerations
- Major business unit responsibilities
- Business unit operating methods
- External partner considerations
- Planned new business units
- Possible new government regulations
- Major technology enablement considerations
- Knowledge transfer and skills management
- Security and privacy considerations
- Predictions of operating environment changes

The Restructuring Project Manager (PM) should prepare a guiding principles list with examples of applying them.

3b. Identify Business Needs & Goals.

This may sound redundant given the guidance obtained in Step 3a, but the revisit is needed to ensure that the mission purpose and business priorities/needs/goals are kept in mind during scenario development, alternatives analyses, and recommendation development. Examples of key business needs and goals include:

- Significantly strengthen the eCommerce sales channel.
- Eliminate supply chain single points of failure.
- Ensure that critical skill sets are preserved/enhanced.
- Increase external provision of basic administrative items.
- Improve data storage resiliency and security.
- Improve real-time global video meeting capabilities.
- Achieve one-day major order turnarounds.

The CRE, PM, and Secretary should then prepare a business goals/needs list with examples.

3c. <u>Develop List of Challenges & Opportunities</u>.

In reviewing the new organization's design, it is important to identify challenges and opportunities in making changes to structure and function. A good way to do this is to use the SWOT evaluation method. A SWOT analysis identifies the internal and external strengths and weaknesses of an area of the organization or overall.[15] An example layout is:

Time	Area	Internal		External	
Near-Term (1-3 Years)	Strengths	1. 2.	3. 4.	1. 2.	3. 4.
	Weaknesses	1. 2.	3. 4.	1. 2.	3. 4.
	Opportunities	1. 2.	3. 4.	1. 2.	3. 4.
	Threats	1. 2.	3. 4.	1. 2.	3. 4.
Long-Term (4-10 Years)	Strengths	1. 2.	3. 4.	1. 2.	3. 4.
	Weaknesses	1. 2.	3. 4.	1. 2.	3. 4.
	Opportunities	1. 2.	3. 4.	1. 2.	3. 4.
	Threats	1. 2.	3. 4.	1. 2.	3. 4.

---

[15] More information on SWOT Analysis is available at https://www.investopedia.com/terms/s/swot.asp.

Example opportunities include complimentary skill sets, service offerings, logistical methods, and customer base. Example weaknesses include significantly different cultures and major system designs, unhealthy union relations, or lack of configuration and data management standards.

3d. <u>Develop Initial Enterprise Architecture Design</u>.

With the CEO and CRE guidance and results of prior steps in mind, the CRE and CEA should lead an architecture discussion with the ESC and RMT on options for changes to structure and function. General design approaches should be incorporated (e.g., centralized vs decentralized, flattening, outsourcing, insourcing, use of artificial intelligence, and security shells). This initial EA design should be documented as both a narrative description and an overview diagram, as shown in Section 2.2. Many people are visual learners and the overview diagram is helpful in showing business units and their functions and relationships, as well as the organization's data collections, systems, and infrastructure.

3e. <u>Create a Prioritized Actions List</u>.

From input received during the prior steps, the CRE, RMT, and WGs should develop a draft list of prioritized actions that each CXO and business unit will need to take in the near-term (next 3 months) and long-term (next 2 years). The CRE and PM should get feedback from the ESC and RMT and then use this list in creating the restructuring schedule in the next step.

3f. <u>Create an Implementation Schedule & Tracker</u>.

The Restructuring Implementation Schedule and Tracker can be created using commercially available software. As mentioned, Agile project management methods are recommended because they promote rapid, highly iterative modular activities (sprints) and their outputs in a way that allows for direction changes or restarts if they are needed, without upsetting the entire project. The project schedule should show each sprint, the sprint leader, the timeframe, dependency links to other sprints, and the outputs (products or services). A general example is as follows:

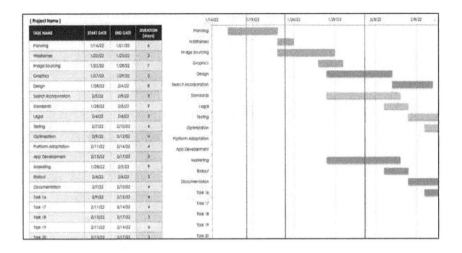

Examples of the output of a sprint include migrating a database, aligning two related workflows, shutting down a duplicated supply warehouse, shifting IT system hosting to a new data center, and combining financials onto one system.

3g. <u>Create a Business/Tech Restructuring Roadmap</u>.

It is critical that the combined organization has a sequenced schedule of actions as described in the prior step, but this has to be accompanied by a sequencing plan that is focused on addressing gaps and overlaps in business units and enabling technology assets. Here are examples of a business and technology alignment roadmap.[16]

---

[16] Source: https://www.researchgate.net/figure/Service-Transition-Technology-Roadmap_fig1_261166955

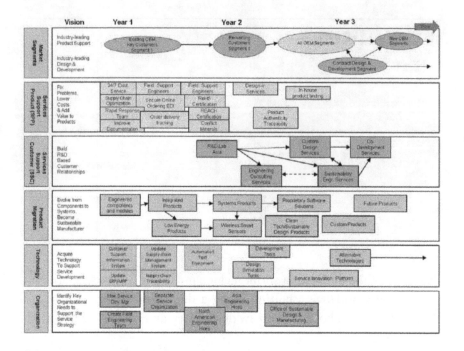

3h. Create Several Comparative Analyses

The details of the restructuring roadmap should be identified through a series of comparative analyses – one for each domain (strategic initiatives, business activities, data collections, systems/applications, and infrastructure). These analyses should show the types and formats of assets and activities in each domain. The following are examples of each:

Strategic Initiatives Comparison
This comparison will be mostly qualitative, not quantitative. The objective is to identify and highlight the most important goals and initiatives for each organization. These objectives may not align, but there might be some relationships that can be beneficial when the organizations are combined. For example, if one organization was trying to increase its customer base and the other organization was trying to increase repeat business (customer loyalty) there may be some commonality in related initiatives. The following is an example of a simple layout that can support comparison:

Strategic Goals Comparison					
Company X			Company Y		
Strategic Goal X-1 Increase Market Share by 5% in 2 Years			Strategic Goal Y-1 Increase Repeat Customers by 15% This Year		
Initiative XA	Initiative XB	Initiative XC	Initiative YA	Initiative YB	
Strategic Goal X-2 Eliminate Supply Chain Single Suppliers in 1 Year			Strategic Goal Y-2 Launch New Financial System This Year		
Initiative XD	Initiative XE		Initiative YC		
Stratetegic Goal X-3 Decrease Injury Lost Days By 20% This Year			Strategic Goal Y-3 Outsource Online Sales Channel		
Initiative XF	Initiative XG		Initiative YD	Initiative B	Initiative C

Business Activities Comparison

This comparison lists the types of major functions and workflows in each business unit of both organizations. The same categories should be used as much as possible to promote comparison and identify targets for consolidation. If the restructuring strategy is to totally absorb the selling organization, there still may be some best-in-class methods and assets that are worth bringing into the acquiring organization. In a merger of equals that are in the same sector, each business unit, asset, and workflow need to be assessed as to which will be retained – and how long parallel operations should be allowed. The following is an example of a business activity comparison diagram:

Business Activities Comparison		
Type	Company X	Company Y
Admin & Collaboration		
Data Management		
eCommerce Channel		
Facilities Management		
Finance & Accounting		
Human Resources		
IT Systems & Security		
Legal		
Logistics & Distribution		
Manufacturing		
Planning		
Product Development		
Sales & Marketing		

It is helpful to add specifics on products and standards that am activity uses. This will support decisions and methods for combining or retiring all or part of an activity.

Data Collections Comparison

This comparison should list the types and formats of large and small (but important) data collections in each organization. By using the same set of data categories for both organizations, there will be an initial identification of which data collections use the same software applications, products, and standards – which will make data migration much easier. An equally valuable reveal is which data collections use proprietary data formats and applications, which may make migration more difficult, or impossible without retaining the proprietary product. The following is an example of a data comparison:

Data - Comparative Assessment			
Type	Organization X	Organization Y	Standard
Storage Area Network	X		SNMP
Storage Area Network		X	WEBM
Data Warehouse - ERP Vendor A	X		Vendor A Proprietary
Data Warehouse - ERP Vendor B	X	X	Vendor B Proprietary
Inventory Database		X	SQL
Inventory Database	X		Vendor C Proprietary
Supply Chain Database	X	X	Vendor D Proprietary
ERP Finance Database	X		Vendor E Proprietary
ERP Finance Database		X	Vendor F Proprietary
HR Database	X		Vendor E Proprietary
HR Database		X	Vendor F Proprietary
Spreadsheet Collection	X		.xls
Spreadsheet Collection		X	.xlsx
Shared Drive Files	X	X	Misc
Legal Files Database	X		Vendor G Proprietary
Legal Files Database		X	Vendor H Proprietary
Misc. Database	X		JSON
Misc. LinuxDatabase		X	.tar
Misc. Access Database		X	.mdb, .xml
Misc. Flat Files	X	X	Misc
Media Vault	X		.wpl, .wav
Outlook Email Database	X		.msg
Gmail Email Database		X	.vsf
Apple Mail Database		X	.emlx
Image File Database	X	X	.jpeg

In addition to a comparative list, models of data collections are needed to show structure and function using established standards like the Unified Modeling Language (UML). Entity-Relationship and Data Flow Diagrams are very helpful, as is a Data Dictionary and Object Library. Perhaps the organization has a Master Data Management program with standards.

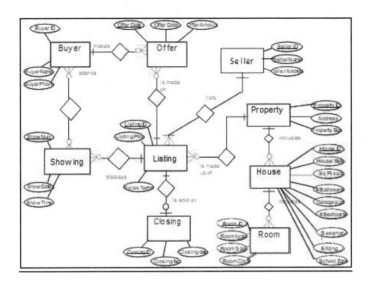

I have found, even recently, that there unfortunately is no software product (tool) that can automatically scan a system, network, or cloud computing environment and produce a plain-language list of items, such as databases, applications, and/or systems. Such a list would likely be in the form of a spreadsheet that consists of rows for each item that the scan finds. The columns would provide a management-friendly description of the purpose and functions of each item, as well as attributes for the owner, the administrator, vendor product names and versions, security/privacy sensitivity levels, who the user groups are, and sharing relationships with other items. At best, today's tool-based scans produce technical data (e.g., machine number, version code, and IP address).

Therefore, staff business and technology analysts are needed to assemble the most useful inventories of data and information on workflows, data collections, applications, websites, networks, facilities, and capital assets. These are the most valuable in supporting management decision-making. Eventually, more advancements in the abilities of AI search and logic will enable tools that can produce management-friendly inventories and a host of analyses and visualizations.

Category	Item Name	Purpose	Owner	Administrator	Sensitivity	Product(s)	ATO Date	Related D	Related A	Related S	Users
Data											
	Item D1										
	Item D2										
Applications											
	Item A1										
	Item A2										
Systems											
	Item S1										
	Item S2										

Systems/Applications Comparison

This comparison should list the types and formats of systems and software applications that are used to support business activities and data management functions. System interface diagrams, as shown below are helpful in understanding the hardware and software components in business and technology systems, to include robots, heavy equipment and mobile capabilities that are owned, leased, or subscribed to.

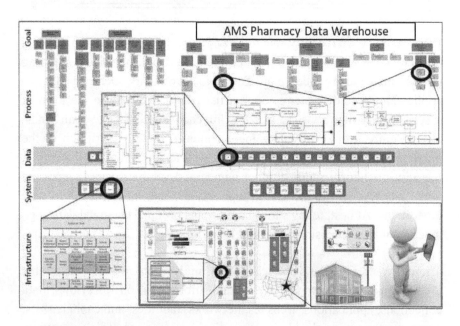

Infrastructure Comparison

This comparison should list the types of facilities, networks, and capital equipment that the organization owns, lease, or subscribes to – along with standards for processes and specification sheets for equipment and building blueprints.

This documentation and the comparative lists should be helpful in deciding which facilities and equipment should be retained, which can be disposed of, and the best timeframe. What goes and stays should be dictated by business goals.

3h. Assemble a Documentation Library.

It is important to create and populate an access-controlled internal repository of the documentation that is used in the restructuring effort. The team may want to lower risk of loss by establishing two repositories, one on a stand-alone computer and locked file cabinet in the meeting area, and a duplicate computer/file cabinet at another operating location.

Phase 4. Restructuring Activities

The first three phases of this restructuring process focused on preparatory and design activities. Phase 4 is where the actual changes to structure and function are implemented.

4a. Create Targeted Working Groups.

There are many (hundreds, perhaps thousands) of actions that need to be taken when bringing two organizations together, especially if they are large and diverse. Even if the merger approach is to operate the acquired organization independently, there are dozens of coordinating actions that need to be accomplished.

To ensure that the proper level of focus and expertise is provided in each action area, targeted working groups (WGs) need to be formed within the Restructuring Team. Each WG should have a group leader identified, who reports to the PM. Some leaders have several WGs under their oversight. The leader should have expertise in their WG area(s) to promote better tracking, decision-making, and solution development.

Each WG's activities are tracked on the Restructuring Project Schedule & Tracker, through quantitative metrics for cost, performance, and schedule that are identified in discussions with the PM and CRE when the WG is being established. Variance levels need to also be identified and stop-light status charts are an easy-to-understand way of presenting progress status (e.g., green means within 10% of target, yellow is within 20% of target, red is above 20% of target).

There will likely be interdependencies between some WGs and these need to be identified before WG establishment whenever possible. These interdependencies should have tracking metrics identified to maintain focus on them.

4b. <u>Start Regular Internal/External Briefings</u>.

Whenever there are major changes in people's work environment, there is tremendous interest, curiosity, and concern... mostly in terms of "what does this mean for me?"

The best way to address concerns and promote a culture of cooperation and accomplishment is to hold regular status briefings and have an online restructuring progress webpage that continually provides information and resources.

Internal briefings will be frequent at first and then settle into a regular rhythm unless a significant problem arises, which is addressed by dedicated solution and status meetings. External briefings are less frequent, and should align with the accomplishment of major milestones and other normal reporting (e.g., quarterly or annual reports).

The CEO should deliver major briefings, assisted by the CRE. The CRE should deliver briefings to the ESC, assisted by the PM. The PM should brief the WG leader group. The Secretary and team analysts should prepare all briefings for review by the CRE or PM prior to being given.

It is important to have an internal webpage that provides answers to frequently asked questions (FAQs), discusses areas of focus or changes to the merger plan, and provides contact information for WG members, stakeholders, and all employees. Including a feature where anyone within the organization can submit a question to the PM will be helpful in maintaining good communications and surfacing areas of concern. Active ongoing engagement by the CRE and PM with key stakeholders is also important – pursued through targeted calls and video meetings. Keeping an ongoing pulse on the merger situation overall can be enhanced when the CRE and PM are talking with individuals and groups frequently.

4c. Set-up Employee Assistance Desk.

Beyond the restructuring internal website, it is a good idea to establish an Employee Assistance Desk (EAD) that is staffed by the HR group and can be accessed by phone or email. Because there will be significant concern (even fear) with some employees over what the restructuring means for them, a robust assistance resource is needed to assuage fears and give correct information on status, guiding principles, and options for employees who may have to make changes in which position they hold with the organization.

Most merger restructuring involves the elimination of duplicated capabilities between the two organizations. This means that some employee positions will be cut, and this is a real source of fear for those who will have that happen. The

There is a significant cultural aspect to restructuring, as employees will be examining decisions through a lens of "that's how much value the leadership places on the staff". In some organizations, the culture was one of strong co-commitment to long-term employment and generous support for re-skilling when position changes occurred. In other organizations, there is more of a transactional culture of high turnover in routinized positions. In organizations with unions, there is a white collar/blue collar ongoing dynamic that centers on skills, wages, stability, and fairness.

Regardless of past cultural histories, the organization should use the merger and restructuring activities as an opportunity to improve employee relations for those who are staying and to be fair (generous) and supportive to those who are leaving.

The EAD can make a big difference in easing people through the restructuring transition, and it is important for the CEO and CRE to openly support the EAD in words and resources.

4d. <u>Hold Daily Team Meetings</u>.

Early in the restructuring program, daily meetings of the RMT and WGs will be necessary. These should be scheduled for a half-hour online with a standardized agenda. The RMT meeting should be chaired by the CRE and the WG meeting should be chaired by the PM or lead member, with notes recorded for both by the Secretary, which are then published after being reviewed by the chair. Additional meetings can be scheduled to discuss specific problems or opportunities as they arise. As the number of remaining actions decreases (usually after a couple of months), the daily meetings can become less frequent. Remember, agile methods call for high rates of iteration among managers, subject matter experts, user reps, and other stakeholders. Recurring and special meetings are what will create that high level of iteration.

4e. <u>Track Progress & Remove Obstacles</u>.

It is important to continually track progress on identified tasks, and to resolve problems as they arise. Tracking can be facilitated by creating a Restructuring Project Implementation Schedule & Tracker using commercial software (described in 3f). Including a quick progress review in the daily meetings is recommended, as is quick reaction to new problems as they arise. This is most important early in the restructuring process, but as changes for structure and functions are made, the remaining activities decrease and so should new problems, if proper assessment and solutioning is done. If not, there will be persistent area that are sub-optimized or totally dysfunctional, which often effects related processes and systems, and my lead to a major problem with restructuring, even overall failure of the merger effort. Continued CEO and CRE involvement will reduce the risk of such failures.

4f. <u>Identify Restructuring End & Lessons Learned</u>.

As with any project, there needs to be an official start, tasks/sprints, the finish, and a recap. Maintain a clear understanding of these project phases keeps the participants organized and engaged, otherwise the project becomes an endless crawl of low-value achievements… a backwater that reduces the credibility of leaders.

That said, no project is without stragglers or off-shoots that will linger or endure beyond the project finish. No problem, just identify those activities that will continue beyond the finish and place them in either a separate post-restructuring project or another program area. The restructuring project's key personnel (CRE, PM, WG Leaders, and Secretary) can be reassigned to other activities near the end and can stop their work once the lessons-learned recap is done.

The lessons-learned recap is a very important activity, as it encourages leadership to take an honest look at how things went with the restructuring project – what went well, what didn't, what they would do differently in other similar projects. To maximize objectivity, the CEO and CRE should bring in an independent external consultant with significant M&A experience. The findings of the lessons learned review should be shared with the ESC and RMT, with targeted sharing with cognizant WGs and key stakeholders.

3.4 Moving Forward (Post-Restructuring)

Some organizations have a growth strategy that includes making a number of acquisitions each year and these all need to be aligned with the baseline enterprise architecture of the organization. Hopefully, the results of each acquisition will achieve the stated goals of doing the deal, as tracked by the CEO, Board, and other senior leaders.

Unfortunately, there are many examples of organizational leaders "gaming" the interpretation of the in-progress status and/or final results of an acquisition and merger. Reasons include hubris, fear, misplaced competitiveness, and incompetence. Whatever the reason, any skewing of results is not helpful to the health of the organization and should not occur. Confident, competent, visionary leaders are able to state situations for what they are, admit mistakes, share credit, include diverse viewpoints, and present a balanced viewpoint of future opportunities.

As mentioned before, programs are ongoing organizational activities, while projects are time-specific efforts to achieve specific outputs or outcomes. Projects have a beginning and an end... most effective when done in days, weeks, or months. Outputs are usually tangible details (e.g., number of votes cast for a candidate), while outcomes are the overall result (the candidate won the election). Outcomes are more important than outputs, but it is the accumulation of the outputs that leads to the outcome.

With regard to mergers and acquisitions, the desired outcome usually is a better, more capable organization. The output results of specific restructuring activities hopefully leads to this outcome. If not, the organization needs to understand what was wrong with the fundamentals of the deal, the design of the restructured organization, or in the execution of restructuring tasks. The aforementioned lessons learned will reveal some of this, if done properly, but other indicators of a successful outcome may not be evident for several years because the restructured business units may need to become proficient in new methods, employees with new positions need time to adapt and thrive, and customers may need time to adjust to new services, products, and brand management approaches. In any case, the merged organization should continue to evolve and adapt in response to internal and external changes, not just the restructuring plan.

Section 4

Special Cases

Section 4

Special Cases

In this section I will briefly discuss several special cases of M&A, including particular considerations in restructuring a consortia or a holding company, both of which are types of collections of companies. The multi-organizational participation in a merging supply chain is also discussed.

4.1 Architecture for Consortia

A consortia is a group of organizations that are legally bound in specified ways by contract. Consortia exist in all sectors: public, private, and non-profit. General examples include:

- Colleges that cross-list classes
- Government agencies that promote food safety
- Non-profit consortia that promote green energy
- Industry consortia that promote video streaming
- Telecom consortia that promote internet connectivity
- Corporations that make aircraft together
- Governments that allow Visa-free cross-travel
- Corporations/agency that participate in a power grid

OPEC, Airbus, the European Union, NATO, Big Ten Academic Alliance, and Five College can be considered to be examples of consortia. Their legally binding document types are:

OPEC	Declaration of Cooperation
EU / NATO	Government Treaty
Airbus	Treaty & Contract
Five College	Contract

Holistic EA methods do not change for consortia, as the top-level cube shows member organizations (top), normal functional domains/threads (front), and independent or coordinated services are shown on the side face, as follows:

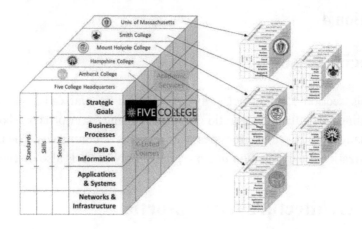

4.2 Architecture for Holding Companies

Holding companies are a bit different from consortia in that while they are a collection of organizations, the binding relationship is that the parent (umbrella) company owns the subordinate companies and oversees management decisions, but does not operate them directly. The umbrella company may be an investment group, a multi-sector conglomerate, or a single sector corporation. Subordinate companies can be aligned or diverse in their mission purposes. Examples of umbrella companies include 3M, Carlisle, Honeywell, General Electric, Unilever, L3 Technologies, and Berkshire Hathaway. HEA methods are the same in holding company M&A activities.

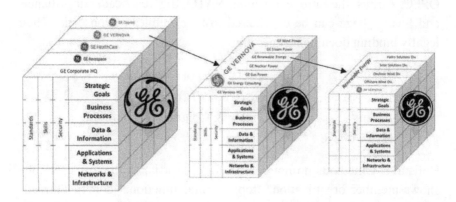

4.3 Architecture for Supply Chains

A supply chain is a cooperative group of organizations that participate in the process of creating and delivering tangible products. Supply chains link value chains (value chains are the linked processes within an organization that create or enhance the value of a product or service). Suppliers in a supply chain are ranked by tier, with first-tier suppliers supplying directly to the client, second-tier suppliers supply to the first-tier, etc. An example of a supply chain is the automobile manufacturing process, whereby several dozen companies contribute raw materials or individual parts to an assembling company, which creates the final product and sends them to dealerships to sell and service. Another example is a big-box retail supply chain wherein hundreds of products are shipped to stores and online fulfillment warehouses with coordination on reorder levels and logistics coming from a common information system, that is linked to the point-of sale system so that intake and outflow are in sync.

The key links in a supply chain are the product's design and participation standards. Synchronization is needed to ensure that the supply chain is both functional and efficient, done through tightly and loosely coupled processes. Only parts of a participating organization are involved in the supply chain.

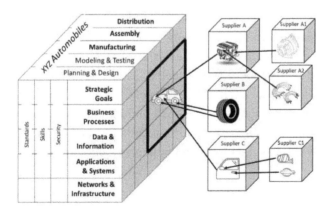

4.4 Architecture for Start-Ups

A start-up is an organization that has been formed in the recent past and is usually not large or diverse. That said, some start-ups that have significant resources (usually from investors or a parent company) can grow quickly and begin to face the problems of managing a diverse group of product and sales units along with administrative and logistical functions.

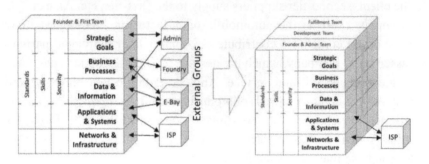

Start-up organizations usually begin with a founder and several initial employees. Funding comes from the founder or an investor and work is done at one location – sometimes the founder's garage or basement (think Apple, Amazon, Mattel). Inexpensive external service groups are initially used as products and services are developed, tested, and delivered.

As products and services mature, and sales increase, the organization begins to create internal business units to lower costs and gain control over processes that may need to be aligned or customized. Some external groups may be able deliver more sophisticated, secure services at a lower cost point (e.g., internet services, office financials/HR, eCommerce channels). The role of Holistic EA is to establish and maintain an overview of the growing organization and promote standards for sharing and reuse across the business units as they form and mature. Documentation is boring but essential.

Section 5

An Illustrative Story

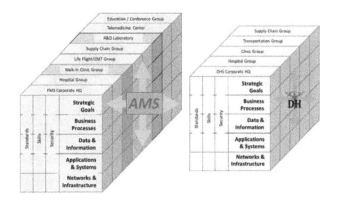

Section 5

An Illustrative Story

This story is presented to illustrate how organization-wide views, concepts, and methods can be applied to merger and acquisition activities.

The two organizations are fictitious privately held companies in the health care industry. The buying organization (Apex Medical Services - AMS) is a growing multi-state public corporation that owns and operates a network of seven hospitals, twelve clinics, three testing lab sites, and a supplies distribution warehouse. The selling organization (Danbridge Health - DH) is a smaller single-state family-owned corporation that operates three hospitals, six clinics, a warehouse, and an ambulance service.

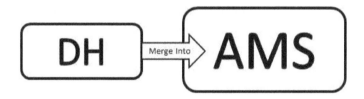

This acquisition will benefit AMS by expending service coverage into a neighboring State and increasing market share in a region where other direct competition is increasing. The sale will benefit Danbridge Health in that the founder died and the inheritants do not want to continue the business. Challenges include the pre-deal valuation of DH by both parties as well as post-deal restructuring and knowledge transfer into AMS. There is a surprise twist that AMS has to deal with since they are a public corporation, but I won't give that away now.

Scene 1: We Want to Sell

On a rainy Monday in March, Julia Danbridge-Smith walked with her family from their lawyer's office toward her car. She turned to her brother Andrew and said, "Let's talk tomorrow about dad's business". He said "Sure, I'll come over after work." They had just heard the reading of their father's Will and learned that he left them ownership of the longtime family business, Danbridge Health (DH), which is an umbrella corporation for several hospitals and clinics in the State.

Julia had coffee and scones ready for Andrew when he arrived and they sat down at the kitchen table. "Dad was a wonderful doctor and did so much for our community" she said. "You are a great doctor too, but I saw how much time it took for dad to run the corporation and I wonder if that is what you want to do too. I don't want to do that stuff, but maybe you do."

Andrew stirred his coffee and said "Thanks Julia, your support is important to me. I miss dad so much already and I respect what he built, but my real happiness is in spending time with family, friends, and patients. I don't want to run a big business; it's a huge time commitment that would take away from what I value most. Also, I think that the best path to continuing quality care is for the business to become part of a bigger health care system that has the resources to afford the newest equipment and top practitioners." Julia gazed out the window, "You know, I think that mom would understand if we put the company in better hands." Andrew said "I think so too. Would it be ok if I talk to the lawyer about the best way to find the right buyer?" Julia clasped Andrew's hand and said "Yes, do that, thanks again for your understanding."

The next morning Andrew left a message with the family lawyer, Craig, asking for an appointment at the end of the week for him and Julia. It was Friday late afternoon when they walked into Craig's office and he said, "Hi Julia and Andrew, I want to say again that I am sorry about your father's passing and am grateful for his work in building this State's best group of hospitals and clinics." "Thank you" said Julia, "Andrew and I talked, and we don't want to run that organization, our priorities are elsewhere." Andrew added "That's right, but the State needs highly available top-quality health services, so we want these capabilities to continue through a more capable group. We need you to find a couple of suitable groups and get the company ready to be presented."

Craig leaned forward in his chair and said "I understand what you want and why. My specialty is trusts and wills, not mergers and acquisitions, but I would be happy to lead a team that can do what you ask. Your father's company is a Limited Liability Corporation and he was sole owner. There was no stock issued. His will indicates that your mother was to inherit all of his estate and their assets, and if she pre-deceases him, which she did, that each of you will receive half of the estate and assets, which includes Danbridge Health, LLC.

It will take about a month to get a package ready and I can be designated by you two as Acting CEO of DH if you want that during the interim, with you two as co-Board Chairmen so that you have the final say on all matters. I will also contact a couple of M&A experts for advice.

Andrew said, "Please do that" which Julia echoed as they left.

Discussion

An organization "comes into play" by being offered for sale or when executive control can be gained (a friendly or hostile takeover). This occurs for various reasons, including owner disagreement, retirement, or death, financial weakness, excess breakup value, uniquely attractive intellectual property, aging infrastructure, stock price changes, or a government ruling.

In this story, the owner dies and the inheritants do not want to run the company. I chose a small single-owner company to simplify the story and to illustrate how the lack of an organization's ability to effectively tell its story and show value becomes a big problem when trying to attract buyers. If the way it's run is mostly in the head of the owner, then it's not easy to share and is totally lost if that person becomes unavailable. Second-hand views and stacks of files are not very effective during the pre-deal evaluation (due diligence) by potential buyers. The prospective buyers want/need the context and accurate specifics on the organization's strategic direction, legal obligations, audits, business plans, workflows, data collections, systems, staff/skills, and facilities.

In this example, the owner unexpectedly dies and a valuation review had not been recently done. It is good that the owner has an attorney who the family trusted and could step in as Acting CEO when requested and pull together a team to get the company ready for sale. This attorney understood the desires of the inheritors and had executive control with direct access to company employees, assets, and information so that he could coordinate how the organization would be valued and presented during due diligence and purchase negotiations.

Scene 2: Hey Look at This

On a sunny Wednesday morning in early April, Jim Vargas, the CFO of Apex Medical Services (AMS), noticed that the employee parking lot at the headquarters office was nearly full as he walked over to the office of CEO Kristin Marsten. "Thanks for making time to see me this morning he said, I have something to show you. Before that, did you notice that the lot is nearly full? This is wonderful – certainly a change from the last two years as we have been dealing with the turbulence of the pandemic."

Kristin responded "Yes, I did notice that, and seeing people in their offices and the meeting rooms is indeed wonderful. I understand that many of the staff want to continue remote work, but medical services is largely an in-person profession. That said, I believe that we have to accept that telework and expanded telemedicine are here to stay, and I think that we are starting to adapt nicely to that. So, what did you want to show me Jim?"

Jim tapped the screen of his tablet and handed it to Kristin. "Take a look at this."

Kristin's eyes grew wide as she examined the image. "Wow, the Danbridge kids have decided to sell their dad's business. You know, I started my career with Danbridge Health as a staff attorney just after graduating from law school. I stayed with them for eight years before coming over to AMS as deputy chief counsel. Bill Danbridge was a wonderful, personable doctor and grew his practice with the same compassion over fifty years. The Danbridge group was the first multi-hospital and clinic network in the mid-State area, and their internal patient transportation service was another first."

Kristin continued, "I guess that Julia and Andrew don't want to run the business. Well, upon seeing this, my first reaction is that this may be a good expansion opportunity for us, but we will need to check out all aspects of Danbridge and their broker's valuation. I believe that DH is a sole proprietor LLC, but let's confirm that and what the SEC rules are for a publicly-traded corporation like ours buying a small privately-owned LLC. Because they listed the company with XYZ Brokerage and put it out nationally, I'm sure that there will be interest from several regional and national HMOs. Jim, thanks for bringing this to me, please call a meeting of the executive team for this afternoon at 4pm so that we can get the discussion going. We may need to move fast so make sure that everyone understands that this is a high priority confidential internal meeting."

"Will do" said Jim as he took back the tablet and started out the door. "And I will pull together some data on DH's financials, services, and media items over the past five years."

Kristin added, "I am going to call the Board of Directors' secretary now who can let Chairman Palmer know about this opportunity. He can let the other Board members know if he chooses to, though I will ask him to consider holding off for a few hours while we get our position together – then we can get their feedback. Remember, mums the word for everyone!"

Discussion

Sometimes an organization has unique value and will attract potential buyers as soon as it comes on the market. In this case we have a small HMO that is well established in an otherwise underserved location. This HMO provides quality services, has little debt, and no big legal issues. No wonder a larger HMO in a nearby State may quickly try to confirm the condition/value of the target organization and make an offer. Getting a short period of exclusive access to the target organization is a wise move if it can be done, as other buyers are already queuing up.

I made the potential buyer a publicly-traded corporation to be able to include the dynamics of a Board of Directors, shareholder groups, and the Security and Exchange Commission. M&A is a highly regulated, highly lucrative business area that sees tens of thousands of deals done globally each year. Unfortunately, many pre-deal valuations are incomplete/inaccurate, and post-deal restructuring of the organizations does not go well, so value can be reduced.[17] [18]

I have been a part-time college professor for over two decades and I always tell my students that there is "the world of the ideal" (class readings and discussions) and the "world of the real" (what actually happens in organizations every day). Many M&A books, including this one, talk about three general phases: (1) pre-deal due diligence; (2) negotiating/signing the merger or acquisition deal; and (3) post-deal restructuring in combining the two organizations. In the real world, any of these phases can be shortened, lengthened, or skewed due to incomplete assessments, executive hubris, government regulatory rulings, lawsuits, media coverage, market changes, new bidders, and other situations.

Every M&A event is unique, yet it is important to understand the standard financial and legal concepts and methods that shall/should be followed.

---

[17] https://dealroom.net/blog/reasons-why-mergers-and-acquisitions-fail. 10 Common Reasons Why Mergers and Acquisitions Fail

[18] Forbes (2019). Most Mergers Fail Because People Aren't Boxes. https://www.forbes.com/sites/forbescoachescouncil/2019/06/24/most-mergers-fail-because-people-arent-boxes/?sh=308905235277

What also needs to be understood is how the two organizations actually function at the macro and micro levels. An interesting article on this was published in *Forbes* in 2019 entitled "Most Mergers Fail Because People Aren't Boxes".[19] The failure to understand cultural, policy, and methodological differences between the organizations is a significant contributor to M&A restructuring problems.

Scene 3: We May Want to Buy

At 4pm the same Wednesday in April, CEO Kristin Marsten welcomed the following AMS executives to her office:

Richard Smith	Chief Operating Officer
Jim Vargas	Chief Financial Officer
Gabriella Lumella	Chief Counsel
Marty Pulman	Chief Enterprise Architect
Sandy Wolford	Chief Human Capital Officer
Dennis Button	Chief Medical Officer

Thank you for coming to this short-notice meeting," said Kristin. Earlier today, Jim let me know that Danbridge Health is in play as of this morning, with XYZ as their brokerage. This may be a good expansion opportunity for us and there will likely be several offers from regional and national HMOs, so I wanted to get your views quickly. I called Board Chairman Palmer and he agrees that this is an interesting opportunity that needs to be moved on quickly and he also agreed with my recommendation to wait to inform the full board for a couple of days while the executive team does the initial analysis. Jim has already pulled information on DH together so he will start"

Jim Vargas (CFO) activated the room's large smart screen and pulled up a slide with high level information on Danbridge Health. "DH was founded in 1964 by Dr. William Danbridge to fill a void in the availability of

---

[19] https://www.forbes.com/sites/forbescoachescouncil/2019/06/24/most-mergers-fail-because-people-arent-boxes/?sh=234218025277

primary and advanced medical services in the central mountainous area of his state." They currently operate 3 hospitals, 6 clinics, a supply center, and a patient transportation service. Their headcount is roughly 360 people and annual gross revenue is in the $50M range."

Richard Smith (COO) followed, "Unless there is a hidden toxic element, we will likely want to buy DH if only to prevent a larger HMO from doing so and creating significantly more competition in this region if they launch more locations and services."

Dennis Button (CMO) then spoke, "I agree with Richard, DH had limited resources that caused them to emphasize the provision of basic services and referring out advanced and special cases to other in-State and next-State-over providers, including us. If a well-funded HMO becomes owner of DH, they will have a geographic foothold next to our tri-State primary operating area. They would likely expand services and will stop referring patients to us. DH has a good medical staff and fairly current facilities. I don't know of any major lawsuits, but I will defer to Gabriella on that. So, I don't know of any "toxic elements" that would harm our group if we bought them."

Sandy Wolford (CHCO) said, "I agree with Dr. Button that DH has a competent, well performing medical staff. While they are strongest in their ER and family practice areas, these would be complimentary to our services in the same areas and will also be valuable in our growing telemedicine services. Their ambulance service would be a new gain for us too."

Marty Pulman (CEA) said, "I will make my team available to support scenario modeling and business/technology analyses when you are ready for that and when we are given access to their managers and systems for due-diligence."

Gabriella Lumella (CC) said, "I will look for legal issues."

Kristin, leaned back in her chair and said, "Thank you for your insights. I want to establish a due-diligence team tonight, with selected staff from each of your teams. They each need to maintain strict confidentiality. I want Richard to run the team and each of you to participate and support. I want Gabriella to reach out to XYZ brokerage following this meeting to let them know that we are interested and want to begin due-diligence as soon as possible, and that we are prepared to sign NDAs and pay a refundable deposit of $5 million to obtain exclusive bargaining rights for the next two weeks. This group will meet every day in this room for a working lunch until the deal is done or over."

An hour after the meeting, Richard and Gabriella stopped by Kristin's office to say that they had already contacted the XYZ brokerage and expressed our interest in the acquisition and our desire to obtain exclusive review and offering rights for the next two weeks. XYZ's representative acknowledged these things and said that they would be back to us tomorrow morning.

At 11am on Thursday, the XYZ broker (Brenda Foster) called Richard, who linked in Gabriella, and informed them that DH was pleased that AMS was interested in the acquisition but would not grant an exclusive period for due-diligence and offers. DH wanted to be supportive of AMS and was prepared to sign NDAs and allow DH to begin due-diligence on Friday afternoon. Richard confirmed that this was fine with DHS and to send the NDAs over as soon as was possible. Richard and Gabriella notified Kristin by phone, and she re-emphasized that moving fast would be essential to winning the deal, so a fast moving due-diligence team was a must.

Richard and Gabriella sent an email to the other executive team members after the call with Kristin and asked them to identify the due-diligence analysts in each area by 2pm that afternoon and there would be an executive meeting at 4pm.

The executive group gathered in Kristin's office, where Kristin opened with, "Thanks for assembling the due diligence team so quickly. Gabriella contacted the XYZ brokerage with our desire to get an exclusive two-week evaluation and negotiation period, but DH turned that down, so we will have to keep moving fast to determine if this acquisition is what we want to recommend to the Board. Richard, as the due diligence team leader, please take us through what you know so far, then I want your views."

Richard (COO) said, "No red flags yet and I don't blame DH for rejecting our exclusivity request – they understandably want to attract several prospective buyers who will bid up the purchase price. But to really maximize that price, they will have to be able to show that they are well run, have future growth potential, have their financials in order, can merge similar services, and there are no big legal issues. Let's go around the table to get a quick take on your findings, views, and concerns."

Gabriella (CC) went next, "On the legal side, DH has a malpractice case pending and settled another one last year, but otherwise does not have any big legal issues. They are properly filed as a sole-owner Limited Liability Corporation in the State of DA and there are no liens or tax issues I could see."

It was then Jim Vargas' (CFO) turn. "I was able to get some general financial information from publicly-available tax and filing databases. I confirmed the asset list we have pulled together and that their gross revenue is in the $50M range. I don't know of any special intellectual property or unique service delivery methods that would further increase their value."

Dennis (CMO) echo'd Bill, "I agree that DH uses standard diagnostic and treatment protocols, and I don't know of any super star practitioners, who would change DH's valuation."

Gabriella left the room to take a call from XYZ. Kristin then said, "so who's our competition?"

Richard looked at his tablet and said, "At first glance, I think there are two other contenders: the first is the national HMO All Things Health (ATH) who has deep pockets and pursues a volume-based lowest price services strategy, so they are interested in buying any established HMO that becomes available as that builds their base. The other is Mountain Medical (MM) which is a privately held LLC that was started by a couple of doctors about five years ago and operates in the same area as DH. They have one hospital and a couple of clinics, so finding a way to buy DH would significantly strengthen their staying-power in the mid-State region. If they don't get DH, the successful buyer will look at MM as a small competitor that can only grow organically, which is hard to do, so MM becomes the next takeover target. The magic for MM has been a good professional relationship between their physician-owners and the longtime physician-owner of DH, who is now gone."

Kristin looked at Marty, "What do you need from DH and our team to build a useful picture of DH's structure and functions? I am thinking that this will mostly speak to the post-deal restructuring, and we need to know now if there are going to be big obstacles to bringing our staffs and their different cultures and methods together."

Marty replied, "I have already created a holistic overview model. Looks like a loaf of bread with removable slices, which are the segments of the DH organization at the strategic, business, and technology levels. I need access to their process, data, and system, models to populate the model with more detailed information. Then, we can do a likewise comparison between us and DH that will show gaps and overlaps. It will take a day to build this model if we get cooperation from DH."

Kristin said, "Thanks Marty, please move fast with or without DH's help, so team may need to make assumptions."

Marty replied, "Ok, but I don't want to build a false picture."

Sandy then spoke, "My only addition is that DH has a profit-sharing program, and their employee turnover rate is very low."

Gabriella came back in the room and said, "I just off the phone with XYZ who said that DH thinks that we are a good potential buyer and though they will entertain other offers and info requests, that they are ready now to execute NDA's and set up a video call for 3pm this afternoon with us and XYZ."

"Wonderful!" Exclaimed Kristin. "Please call them back, execute the NDA, and let them know that we are looking forward to the 5pm meeting and will have a list of questions for them, and also tell them we are serious about doing rapid due diligence and hopefully they will be willing to work with us this weekend."

Kristin turned to the group, "Ok team, let's get back together at 2pm with our questions for the meeting with DH an hour later. We need to go over them and ensure we are asking about the right things and present ourselves in a way that builds trust. I will invite Board Chair Palmer to join in too."

Discussion

M&A events are often fast-moving and highly dynamic. Motivations are often different among buyers, the seller and the outside brokers, bankers, lawyers, and other stakeholders. To some, this M&A event is just another financial deal among many they are doing, but to others it's their whole world.

The premise of this book is that organizations have become much more complex, diverse, global, and dependent on technology; yet the expertise areas on a typical M&A team may be lagging in these areas. By not having scalable methods or sufficient assessment capabilities in the technology and culture areas there are significant blind spots that can contribute to failed post-deal merging of the two organizations. Studies from a number of leading universities and consultancies show that more than half of all M&A deals don't result in a well-functioning merged organization.

Developing a holistic view of both organizations is important, and must be done in a way that can be compared to support restructuring decisions and actions. The same modeling framework must be used in order to create the ability to do a "likewise comparison" within and between business units, enabling technologies, data collections, sources of risk, and staff skills and knowledge. This is what CEOs and key executives and managers are often doing in their head instead of with sharable models and narrative documentation.

This organization-wide approach is called Holistic Enterprise Architecture (HEA), which supports executives, managers and staff by recording, modeling, assessing, and sharing within and between all business units using the same approach.

Chief Enterprise Architects (CEAs) are skilled in HEA and have had organization-wide responsibilities. Their HEA approach includes all areas of the organization and can vary in degree of detail or in widening/narrowing the area being looked at.

I would say that Holistic EA is primarily for CEOs, but it can benefit other organizational stakeholders too, especially during major structural changes like with M&A events.

Scene 4: Rapid Due-Diligence

At 2pm Kristen welcomed the executive group back to her office. "Ok, we have an hour to get better prepared for the first call with DH and their broker. Gabriella, how did the NDA signing go?" "No problems" said Gabriella, "I signed for us and sent them scanned copies a half-hour ago, acknowledged just before I came over here. I also sent a video meeting invitation for 3pm." "Great" said Kristin. "Richard, do you have a set of questions to ask them?" "Yes" said Richard as he plugged his tablet into the big smartboard, "Here they are."

We would like copies of:
- Last two year's financial summaries and tax filings.
- Summary of open legal filings by or against DH.
- Hospital and clinic accreditations from the State.
- Land and building titles or lease agreements.
- Outstanding loans, amounts, terms, and lender contacts.
- Strategic and business unit plans.

We would also like to know:
- Descriptions of health service delivery methods.
- Current employee headcount and monthly payroll cost.
- Retiree pension payments and monthly total cost.
- List of owned and leased capital equipment.
- List of IT systems and software applications in use.
- List of data collections and hardcopy record index.

- Disaster recovery plans
- Total asking price and terms for the acquisition of DH.

"That's great," said Kristin. "Does anyone have any other questions for DH? Marty (CEA) said, "Let's ask if they have a high-level architecture repository and if they do, can they give us access." Dennis (CMO) said, "I'd like to know how they coordinate pharmacy services and supplies." Richard (COO) added, "Yes, I'd like to know about their supply chain in general and who their main providers are." Sandy (CHCO) said, "I'd like to know which type of HR system they use and if it includes travel, benefits, and hire-to-retire services." "Ok," said Kristin, "Richard, please add these items to your list and with Gabriella send the DH and XYZ representative a copy as soon as you can. We have about fifteen minutes before the video meeting starts, so let's take a 10-minute break and come back here. I will start for us, and then will turn it over to Richard to go through the list. Each of you can chime in if a question in your area comes up."

A bit before 3pm, Kristin and the group were back in the conference room and Gabriella brought up the video link on the big smartboard. A moment later, the DH conference room camera came on, followed by the XYZ brokerage office. "Hello, I am Kristin Marsten the CEO of Apex Medical Services and we are interested in talking about acquiring Danbridge Health." "Hello, said Brenda Parson, the XYZ lead attorney/broker, "XYZ is proud to offer Danforth Heath on behalf of the owners, Julia and Andrew Danforth, whose father Dr. Richard Danforth founded DH in 1967. They are joined by Craig Harper, the family's attorney." "Hello Brenda, Julia, Andrew, and Craig" said Kristin. "We have been admirers of Dr. Danforth and the DH group for some time. His commitment to quality medical care in the mid-State area is why we are interested in this acquisition, we have the same commitment and don't have facilities in the area."

Brenda spoke, "Thank you Kristin, I appreciate AMS' interest and your awareness that there are several other groups interested in acquiring DH. The next few days will be quite busy, so much for a quiet weekend." "Indeed" said Kristin, and we really appreciate your willingness to give us this time to get a good understanding of DH so we can make a decision soon. Again, we are interested but as I hope you understand, we have to verify the operating status of the company." Andrew spoke up, "Julia and I certainly understand, we are grateful for the interest that AMS has shown, and with the help and advice of Craig and Brenda, we will answer these questions and others that may come up in the next three days. Craig has organized a group of DH executives and physicians who are our subject matter experts and will get the information you want, unless we determine that it is an item that we do not want to disclose at this time… I can't think of anything like that but we may need to say no in some instances." Julia said, "We will be as helpful as we can be."

"Wonderful," said Kristin "We appreciate your openness and support. Richard is our Chief Operating Officer and will lead our due diligence team, with Gabriella working with Brenda and Craig on any legal questions and issues that may come up." You will have a decision from AMS as soon as we confirm DH's status, hopefully by Tuesday at 4pm Central time." "Thank you," said Brenda. "Richard spoke up, "Brenda, can you and Craig stay on the video call for another 15-20 minutes so we can work out the process for sending us information." "Sure," said Brenda. "Fine" said Craig. Kristin said, "Thank you all again, we will leave the room now so that the four of you can talk."

Craig conferred with Andrew and Julia after the call and post-discussion. "Do you have any guidance for me or the DH team as we work with them and Brenda over the weekend?" Julia said, "Let's be honest and open, I don't know of anything that dad did with the business that he and we won't be proud of." Andrew echo'd, "Yes, let's cooperate as much as possible, but I wouldn't share any patient information or private family items."

"Ok." said Craig, "This will be a busy weekend, I will now call the DH team and get them ready for the first team call at 6pm."

Richard assembled the AMS due diligence team at 5:30pm to organize the activities of the next three days and prepare for the 6pm call with the DH team, which Brenda was invited to join.

At 6pm, Richard opened the video call with the DH team, which was gathered in a conference room at their main hospital. Craig opened the conversation with "Hello Team AMS!" Richard said, "Hello Team DH! Well, here we go – this will be a busy three days and on behalf of our

CEO, Kristin Marsten, I want to thank you for your time, knowledge, and viewpoints." Craig said, "We appreciate AMS's interest and are ready to work with you, but I am going to have to ask that we do the inter-team conversations between 8am and 8pm on each day. This will allow our folks to also attend to personal items." "That's fine." Said Richard, can we do team-to-team video calls at 10am and 2pm on Saturday, Sunday, and Monday… with separate focused meetings, calls, and emails between individuals as may be needed?" "Yes." said Craig. "Per the NDA, DH will be recording all of our calls, meetings, and email." "Understood," said Richard. Craig added, "I just sent you a list of the AMS team members/roles."

Craig Harper	Team Lead/Lead Attorney
Janice Brown	Acting CEO/Chief Medical Officer
Herbert Jones	Chief Operating Officer
Yolinda Perez	Chief Administrative Officer
Doug Parker	Chief Information Officer
Victor Kudlow	Chief Counsel
Brenda Forrest	XYZ Broker/Attorney, Advisor
Jack Gardner	M&A Independent Advisor

After the call, Craig went over to the main hospital's executive conference room and spoke to their due diligence team. "Thank you all for staying late on Friday. As you know, Andrew and Julia have put DH up for sale and there already is strong interest. That is a tribute to Dr. Danbridge and he would want our medical company to find a home within a quality provider that has the size and resources to keep our services going for many years to come in the mid-State area that he was so dedicated to. A good prospective buyer contacted our broker who is so interested that they have asked for a short exclusive evaluation period, until Monday afternoon. We want to be supportive of this and going to be working hard over the weekend to answer their questions. Here is the list of questions they have an information that they'd like copies of. It is ok to share this as we have a Non-Disclosure Agreement in place with them and attorneys from AMS, DH, and the broker will be monitoring throughout the process. We will have team-to-team video calls at 10am and 2pm local tomorrow, Sunday, and Monday. We can also do calls and emails in between if they are needed. What I need now is for each of you to assemble as much of the information and answer the questions that you can by 9am tomorrow, when we will meet here to prep for the 10am call. I'll be here until 10pm and back at 8am if you need me."

At 8am on Saturday, the AMS team assembled in their conference room and started going over information on the DH Strategic Plan and two prior years of financials that was emailed to them by Craig the evening before.

At 9am, the DH team assembled. Craig said, "Let's go through the list to see what we have, don't/won't have, or may be able to create." Richard, showed the following slide:

#	Item	Have It	Won't Have	Can Create	Status
1	Strategic Plan.	X			Delivered 4/14
2	Business Plans.	X			Sat. Delivery
3	Last two year's financial summaries and tax filings.			X	Sun. Delivery
4	Summary of open legal filings by or against DH.			X	Sun. Delivery
5	Hospital and clinic accreditations from the State.	X			Sat. Delivery
6	Land and building titles or lease agreements.	X			Sat. Delivery
7	Outstanding loans, amounts, terms, and lender contacts.	X			Sun. Delivery
8	Descriptions of health service delivery methods.	X		X	Sun. Delivery
9	Current employee headcount and monthly payroll cost.			X	Sat. Delivery
10	Retiree pension payments and monthy total cost.			X	Sat. Delivery
11	List of owned and leased capital equipment.			X	Sat. Delivery
12	List of IT systems and software applications in use.			X	Sun. Delivery
13	List of data collections and hardcopy record index.			X	Sun. Delivery
14	Comprehensive disaster recovery plan.		X		***
15	Total asking price and terms for the acquisition of DH.			X	Sun. Delivery
16	High-level architecture repository.		X		***
17	Pharmacy services and supplies coordination.			X	Mon. Delivery
18	Type and functions of HR system being used.			X	Sat. Delivery

Richard said, "We have about a third of what AMS is asking for and all but two of the remaining items can be assembled and sent over later today or tomorrow. There are two business/tech items that we don't have and can't create before Monday afternoon – those are a high-level enterprise-wide architecture and a comprehensive disaster recovery plan.

The 10am team-to-team call started with introductions, then a short discussion on each of the requested items. On item #14 (Comprehensive Disaster Recovery Plan), DH COO Herb Jones said that they had unit-level DR plans, but not a company-wide plan. Richard said that was fine, just send those over. On item #16 (High-Level Architecture Repository) Herb said that they did not have an architecture program or repository, but they do have some system and data models in various online files. Marty (AMS CIO) said that his team could help pull an overview and repository together with Herb's staff through three 4-hour work sessions, which Herb ok'd. Marty added that these products would be left with DH after the due diligence activity. Marty also said that these items are important to see how DH works overall and within/between the business units.

The remaining team meetings on Saturday and Sunday, along with lots of work to locate or create requested items, resulted in DH providing all of the documents to AMS by the 10am Monday team meeting, except for item #15, the terms and asking price for the DH acquisition. For that, Craig said that he would be calling Kristin after the meeting.

The reason that DH did not provide the financial summary was that Craig wanted to go over it with Julia and Andrew prior to sharing it with AMS. The following is the summary:

Type		(Annual $000)	Notes (Annual average over 3 years)
Assets	Cash/CDs	7,860	On Deposit
	Accts. Recv	42,359	Patient + Services Billing
	Capital Eq	12,682	5-Yr Depreciation Schedule
	R&D Grants	1,431	Govt & Private Grants (7)
	Patents	1,203	10-Yr Effective Period
		65,535	
Liabilities	Accts. Pay	9,665	Supplies, External Services
	Salary/Bon.	38,108	Yr Total for all Employees (359)
	Pensions	2,580	Yr Total for Vested Employees (43)
	Owner Profit	3,100	Average Annual Cash Payment
	Loan	3,086	General Ops / 3-Yr Loan Period
	Capital Eq.	8,252	3-Year Purchase Period
	Legal Special	744	Settlement of Legal Cases (3)
		65,535	
Annual Profit x 5 Yrs.		15,500	Projected Earning Potential
Other Assets – Current Value		23,176	Current Liquidatable Assets
Brand Recognition/Loyalty		5,000	Preference for DH Services
Overall Valuation		**43,253**	*Verified by XYZ CPA Firm on 3/4/23*

At noon, Craig spoke with Andrew and Julia on a group video call. "The team calls have gone well and we even have some overviews of the whole business that the AMS team helped us create. Our financial summary is on this slide and the bottom line is that our asking price should be about $45 million. Also, earlier this morning I got two calls from other companies that are interested in evaluating DH, but I told them that we were working with a potential buyer full-time until tomorrow. Both said that they were very interested and would appreciate an opportunity to make an offer." Andrew said, "Which companies are these?" Craig responded, "One is Mountain Medical which is a small local doctor-owned LLC and the other is All Things Health which is a large national HMO with deep pockets." Julia said, "It's nice to see additional interest, but dad would want the new owner to be a quality provider with staying power and commitment to the mid-State area." Craig said, "Mountain Medical has the local commitment, ATH has staying power, and AMS is known for quality services." Andrew said, "we committed to providing AMS with terms and a price this afternoon, so we'd better talk about that." Craig said, "Let me see if I can get Jack Gardner, our independent advisor, to join the call. A minute later, Jack joined the video call and said, "Hello everyone, I'm at my beach cottage seeing what needs to be fixed for the summer season, how can I help?" Craig reviewed the situation and financial summary, then said, "The founder wanted the company to go to a good steward who would stay in the area, so I am thinking of advising Julia and Andrew to put a premium price of $50 million all cash deal with an initial payment of 10% by Tuesday noon and the balance within two weeks." Jack thought for a moment and said, "I think that you should ask for a bit more and cite that other companies are interested... I'd put a $60 million price and all cash deal." They will likely counter-offer and this gives more room for negotiation. I checked on AMS and they have a strong balance sheet and minimal legal issues so you should be open to taking cash equivalents in the deal, like corporate bonds or preferred stock. Be prepared to offer the same deal to MM and ATH this afternoon if AMS does not take this deal."

Craig thanked Jack and said to Andrew and Julia, "So, what do you think?" Andrew said, "I think that it is more important to get a good steward than maximize the price." Julia said, "I agree – a commitment to patients was always dad's priority." Jack said, "Ok, if stewardship is the priority, then I that that Craig is right in recommending a $50 million price with cash or strong equivalents as tender, 10% now and the remainder in a couple of weeks." Craig echo'd "Yes, that's my recommendation". Andrew said, "Julia, I am ok with this, are you?" She said, "Yes I am – please give AMS that offer as soon as you can." "I will" said Craig, and they all signed off the call.

Craig called Jack back and said, "Boy, this has been a busy three days. I wish that DH had done more to gather their documents and create a value and capabilities presentation before the broker listing was done." Jack responded, "Yes, that happens all too often due to a combination of management blind spots and deal-fever. I've seen big corporations that were unable to show their strengths and challenges very well and this resulted in a much lower price and less favorable terms… tens of millions less than if a strong, clear presentation was made." Craig said, "It was interesting that AMS knew what they wanted in terms of company-wide and unit-specific documentation and models. They have an enterprise architecture program that does this for them on an ongoing basis, and they said these products have been really helpful to their planners and operators, especially during two other post M&A onboarding initiatives in recent years." Jack said, "Yes, I've heard about enterprise architecture and I think that it would help most organizations throughout the M&A phases." Craig said, "Thanks for your availability this afternoon, Gabriella and I will be contacting the AMS CEO in a few minutes to go over the terms." "Good luck" said Jack.

Discussion

The story continues to move at a fast pace because a low-problem/high-quality HMO is a valuable acquisition. That said, it is usually management malpractice if no due-diligence is performed (yes, it happens) and part of the role of a Board and key stakeholder groups is to make sure that doesn't happen. Pre-planning by both the selling and buying organizations to have their affairs in order in case a major change or opportunity suddenly appears. The best way that I can think of for an organization to continually have their affairs in order is to stay in compliance with all regulations, maintain a complete/secure records repository, have an effective HEA architecture program with a repository of documents/models/analyses – and be able to present it all.

Scene 5: A Deal, But Not Without Some Drama

The 2pm team-to-team call lasted an hour and focused on closing out a few remaining submissions from DH to AMS. Concurrently, Gabriella worked with Jack and Craig to finalize the financial summaries and a memorandum that provided the $50 million price and cash/equivalent and payment terms that DH wants. These were emailed to the AMS CEO at 3pm. At 3:15pm Gabriella, Craig, and Brenda conferenced together and called Kristen to talk about the valuation and terms memo.

Gabriella started the conversation, "Hello Kristin, Craig is with me, thanks for taking our call – did you receive our valuation and terms?" "Yes I did, and if you'll wait just a moment, I will bridge in our chief counsel Victor Kudlow." Victor joined the call and said, "Hello everyone, I am looking at the valuation and terms document that you sent over a few minutes ago." Kristin added, "I just looked it over and want to say thank you for this and for the outstanding team-to-team cooperation during the go-fast due diligence the past few days." "You are welcome" said Craig. I need to tell you that earlier today we received initial inquiries to our broker by two other companies." Brenda added, "I told them that nothing could be discussed prior to 4pm as there was exclusivity agreement with AMS. One is a small doctor's group and the other is a major HMO. The major HMO begged me not to do a deal before they could make an offer." Kristin said, "Thanks for letting us know, please let me talk privately with Victor and call you back in 10-15 minutes." "That's fine" said Craig and they all hung up.

Victor hurried over to Kristin's office and they called Jason Palmer, AMS Chairman of the Board. Victor stepped out to get Richard who joined them quickly. "Hello Jason" said Kristin, we just received the valuation and terms from Danbridge Heath's chief counsel and they came in at $50 million and wanted an all-cash deal. This is a bit over our valuation, which is at $45 million. They also mentioned during a principals-only call a few minutes ago, that two other companies are interested in making an offer to DH when our exclusivity agreement expires in about 30 minutes." Robert added, "We had a very productive go-fast due diligence period with them over the past three days and no significant problems were identified, but it was tough for them to pull their documentation together." Victor said,

"I agree with Robert's comments and the two other interested companies are Mountain Medical, a small doctor-owned LLC and All Things Health, the major HMO." Jason responded, "Thank you all for the hard work since Friday and I'm glad that we still have some time to be the first to make an offer, if we want to do that. Do we?" Kristin answered, "Yes, we should. Having DH come on the market was unexpected but the price is not outrageous and the acquisition would get us a solid new beachhead in the mid-State area where we don't currently have any activity. Their commitment to quality services is complimentary to ours and there are no significant problems that we could find." "I concur" said Robert. "So do I" said Victor. Jason said, do we pay what they are asking?" Kristin said, "Yes, I would – their revenue stream is strong and their services can grow with our expertise. I think that we could recover the purchase cost within four years, and this deal grows us by about 15% overall, which gets us close to the top-tier HMO group." Jason said, "Ok then, unless there are any other objections, go ahead and do the deal as you described and let me know when it's done." Kristin said, "Will do" and they all hung up.

Kristin leaned forward in her chair and looked at Victor and Robert, "Well, let's get Brenda and Craig on the phone. We have about 15 minutes left on the clock. Victor, please send them an email to say that we are calling and are accepting their price and terms, with payment half in cash and half in preferred stock." "Ok" said Victor. Kristin dialed Brenda and said, "Hello Brenda, we have a deal. AMS will pay the $50 million price for Danfield Health, half cash and half preferred stock. Can we get Craig on the phone to seal this deal?" Brenda said. "That's great, I am dialing Craig now." Craig came on the line and Brenda said, "Hi Craig, I have Kristin, Victor, and Richard on the phone and they support the acquisition deal at the price and terms that your memo stated. Victor is sending you an email to confirm this." Craig said, "That's great and I can tell you that Andrew and Julia will be very happy if AMS acquires their father's company as they have faith that quality medical services will continue to be delivered in the mid-State area and this is what Bill Danfield would have wanted most. Ok, I see the email from Victor with the price and general payment terms. So, I can now tell you that Andrew, Julia, and I talked about other potential offers from MM or ATH and each of them lacked at least one important aspect of what Dr. Danfield would have wanted. So, I can confirm that DH will not be pursuing any additional offers and will accept the AMS offer as stated.

After 4pm I will let those companies know that we are not interested. I will also work with Brenda and Victor over the next couple of hours to get the proper acquisition documents prepared and sent out to all of you. Let's plan on a signing call at 9am tomorrow and a press release at 10am. We will want the 10% half cash, half preferred stock to be sent to Brenda before we sign. The rest is due in two weeks. Any questions?" "None from us" said Kristin. "Thanks Craig" said Victor "I will set up a video call with you and Brenda to start in about 10 minutes. "Thank you everyone" said Andrew. "Thank you everyone" said Julia. Everyone hung up. "Wahoo!" said Kristin, "We have a deal! Ok, Victor let's execute the legalities quickly and correctly. Please check with the SEC on any reporting that we may have to do, or if an approval is necessary before we can actually start to bring DH onboard. Robert, please work on logistics and messaging for the signing video call and press announcement." "I'm on it" said Robert and they departed for their own offices.

On Tuesday morning, the signing and press release went well and featured statements by Andrew and Julia Danfield as well as AMS Chairman Palmer and CEO Marsten. Preliminary restructuring discussions were scheduled to begin at 9am on Wednesday between the AMS and DH teams that got to know each other during the go-fast due diligence effort. These discussions will ensure that leadership can better control the internal and external communications and that the identification of challenges and opportunities can begin.

Discussion

One would think that this is the story's crescendo.... But wait, to me the real action and the real value creation comes in the restructuring phase, but we'll get to that shortly. Ok, a quick disclaimer is in order – this is not a textbook on the financial or legal intricacies of M&A deals – a good source for that is the very comprehensive textbook by Donald DePamphilis.[20] Here, a deal is made because the exclusivity period is ending.

---

[20] Depamphilis, D. (2022). *Mergers, Acquisitions, and Other Restructuring Activities* (11th Edition). Academic Press. ISBN 9780128197820

Scene 6: Coming Together

At 9am Wednesday morning, a team-to-team video call was started with AMS COO Richard Smith making introductory comments. "Hello to our Danfield Health friends. Pending SEC approval, we are looking forward to welcoming you to the Apex Medical Services family! We are very excited about bringing together our two top-quality medical service companies. Dr. Danfield's children have expressed their happiness at the good match between our groups and that the mid-State area will continue to receive top-notch care through the soon to expand AMS group.

I will lead the AMS team and I understand that Herb Jones will lead the Danfield team. Our teams already have a tremendous working relationship that was formed during the above-and-beyond efforts by both groups last weekend, which made this deal possible. I promise that I will be available to each of you and forthright in all dealings as we make preparations to bring our two organizations together. This process will likely have some elements that happen in the next few weeks, while others will take several months or even a year or two"

Richard continued, "I have been through two organizational mergers before and I found that the most important element is clear, consistent communication within and between our teams, as well as with key stakeholders and our customers. Even though we are in the same industry, our companies have different histories, cultures, and methods. Coming together will require commitment and cooperation from everyone. This isn't a hostile takeover thank goodness, this is about AMS expanding to bring DH into our corporate family and continue great health services to the mid-State area. That is a noble cause."

"Herb, would you like to make any opening remarks?" said Robert. Herb responded, "Yes, thank you Robert. As you indicated, Dr. Danfield's children are very happy that AMS is going to become the stable, big umbrella that Danfield Health goes forward under. I also hope that there are no legal impediments or delays to this merger of our organizations, and I appreciate the commitment to transparency and inclusiveness in the many decisions on merging that will be taken in coming months. As you hopefully can understand, the DH team has been together for nearly fifty years. We grew from being a solo practitioner's office to having three hospitals and six clinics today. Our secret to success is a commitment to serve the mid-State area and a population that is proud of their mountain roots and lifestyle. That remoteness is what caused DH to develop one of the nation's first telemedicine services and include all-terrain EMT vehicles in our response and transport fleet. I believe that these capabilities will make a nice addition to the many services and specialty groups that AMS already has. Even though we have some cultural differences, I am confident that if we commit to each other, as Robert said, then we will come together more easily and in a more lasting way. Robert, back to you."

"Thank you Herb." Said Robert. Here is how I'd like to approach these discussions, which cannot be acted upon until the attorneys on both sides say that we are one organization. Again, this should only take a few weeks to finalize. First, I'd like there to be a daily team-to-team (T2T) meeting from 2-4 each afternoon. We may not need all of that time, but let's block it out. Let's also set up an internal webpage later today at both companies, which will become our main communications channel, along with twice-weekly emails from me and Herb."

Robert continued. "Second, we will need to have everyone on the teams sign an extension of the Non-Disclosure Agreements we did last Friday so that it is clearly understood that our T2T work remains confidential. I think that a one-month extension will work and we will send those to everyone this afternoon.

Third, I'd like to use CXO partnerships and service area working groups to identify structure and function in each area. This will be organized through the enterprise architecture framework and methods that AMS has, and which Marty will lead for us. Our CEOs, COOs, and Chief Counsels are already working together, and the next three pairs that I'd like to have begin meeting this afternoon are the CMOs, CHCOs, and

Fourth, our T2T group will have several senior observers and external advisors to provide guidance and recommendations. This includes Chairman Palmer, Brenda Foster of XYZ and Jack Gardner who is an M&A expert. Let's keep them in the know.

Fifth, let's work out differences of opinion between our peer partners whenever possible. There will be plenty of these and one indicator of our effectiveness is that most issues are worked out calmly together. If the manager peers can't work it out, bring it to the CXO partners, and if they disagree, bring it to Herb and me. If we disagree, we will put the issue on a "parking lot list" for resolution by the CEOs and Chair when the merger is legally in effect.

Lastly, if you need additional expertise on an issue, don't contact people outside of the T2T group until you let me or Herb know and discussions with them can't begin until they sign a NDA. Ok, those are the T2T rules, any questions?"

There were none, so Robert continued. "Before we go, I'd like Marty to show us the corporate-wide architecture framework and overview model that will be our common reference for our structural areas and related services. Marty, take it away."

"Thank you Robert" said Marty. He loaded a diagram onto the large AMS smartboard that was also shared to the DH conference room's video screen so both teams could see it.

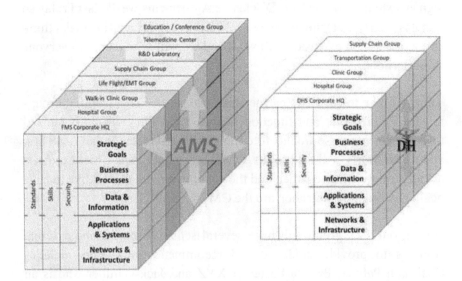

Marty continued, "AMS has been using this "Cube" framework to visualize the overall structure and functions of the company. I took the liberty of also creating a cube framework for the DH organization so we can do a likewise comparison. AMS and DH are medical companies with hospital, clinics, and other services. So, there is lots of overlap that will have to be reduced or eliminated to make sure that the expanded AMS group remains both effective and efficient. Also, the methods we use in each area may be a bit or a lot different, and it will hopefully be clear which one is the best and should be retained going forward. While many of the AMS approaches are likely to go forward, I would think that some of the DH approaches are better and should be what we do in the future. So, we have to look at everything from an effectiveness, efficiency, and alignment set of perspectives. For example, the telemedicine capabilities at DH are better than those at AMS, and DH just bought an integrated CT Scanner/ Robotic Surgery suite that is better than the separate capabilities that AMS has. So, there is a common baseline that we will refer to and I will conduct a more in-depth architecture training session tomorrow and Friday from 7-8am who want more information on this approach.... I think you will find that this will be helpful in your discussions and in maintaining consistency in our preliminary planning. Also, here is an example of an overview diagram for our new Pharmacy Data Warehouse, that is a good way to see relationships between workflows, systems, and facilities. We will be creating one of these for each medical service area."

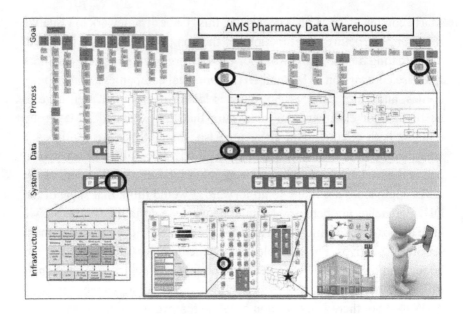

AMS Pharmacy Data Warehouse

"Thank you Marty" said Robert. That's it for this T2T session except I'd like the CMOs to stay on with me and Herb for a few more minutes. Our next meeting is tomorrow from 2-4pm. In the meantime, you can email me and/or Herb with questions.

All of the T2T members except the COOs and CMOs dropped off the video call. Robert opened, "Dr. Button and Dr. Brown, thank you for staying on the call. I hope that Herb would agree that your CMO partnership is particularly important in this merger. We are a pair of medical services companies and maintaining top-level care for our inpatients and outpatients is critical during the transition." Herb said, "I agree 100%." Robert continued, "So, our ask is that you bond quickly and totally so that we hear one medical view whenever possible. The support areas are important, but not as important as patient care. Questions?" "Not from me," said Dr. Brown. "Nor me." said Dr. Button, who added, "I've known Janice since we were both interns at State." Robert concluded with, "Thank you both, Herb, I'm sure we will be talking later today."

Discussion

This final scene closes the story and opens the door to the main message of the book – that having an organization-wide scalable framework for structure and function will greatly assist in restructuring efforts. Organizations are collections of people and things – both have unique aspects that have to be paid attention to. Most people want and need to be part of social and work organizations so they can earn a living and enjoy pursuing their own interests. This is true around the world – a world that is increasingly connected and inter-dependent – a world of organizations – a world of people.

Concluding Thoughts (same as opening thoughts)

Organizations need to understand their structure and functions to be mission effective and cost efficient. A simple, intuitive approach to visualizing structure and function is helpful in achieving this understanding.

If you remember that in any organization goals drive activities, which are enabled by tools, then you can see the key relationships in the Holistic EA Framework. This model can be used with any type of organization and with multiple organizations.

In comparing multiple organizations, you need to use the same framework to have similar presentations of structure and functions. A holistic framework covers all aspects of an organization, which is important when enterprise-wide change and/or improvement is the objective.

In the case of mergers and acquisitions, two organizations are coming together. Even if some parts of either organization are not going to be part of the merger, that change to structure and function has to be understood and factored into other decisions. So, holistic views are needed, and HEA can help.

Mergers and acquisitions are big business in the private sector, lots of money is often involved. Unfortunately, the record of success in combining the organizations is not good. I think that this is because insufficient priority is given to understanding and documenting structure and function. Every organization changes all the time, so it is a moving target as you seek understanding. This makes it more difficult, but still doable if a HEA approach is used. If it is decided that such understanding is not needed, then you are flying blind.

Appendix A

Glossary of Terms

Actionable. EA documentation and data that is useful to executives, managers, and support staff for resource planning and decision-making.

Acquisition. The purchase of something. In the case of mergers and acquisitions, it refers to the purchase of an organization by another one.

Agile Methods. An approach to project management that emphasizes short activity periods (sprints) lots of interchange with stakeholders (iteration), and rapid development, then improvement of outputs/products.

Architecture. A systematic approach that organizes and guides design, analysis, planning, and documentation activities.

Architecture Segment. A part of the overall EA that documents one or more lines of business, including all levels and threads.

Artifact. An EA artifact is a documentation product, such as a text document, diagram, spreadsheet, briefing slides, or video clip. EA artifacts document EA components.

Artificial Intelligence. The ability of a computer or robot to perform tasks associated with intelligent beings such as problem solving, perception.

Blockchain. A digitally distributed, decentralized, public ledger that exists across a network, often the global Internet.

Business Case. A collection of descriptive and analytic information about an investment in resource(s) and/or capabilities.

Business Domain. The second level in the hierarchical Holistic EA Framework that contains assets and activities related to products/services.

Business Unit. A part of an organization that performs a function.

Capital Planning. The management and decision-making process associated with the planning, selection, control, and evaluation of investments in resources, including EA components such as systems, networks, knowledge warehouses, and support services for the enterprise.

Change Management. The process of setting expectations and involving stakeholders in how a process or activity will be changed, so that the stakeholders have some control over the change and therefore may be more accepting of the change.

Chief Executive Officer (CEO). The head of an organization, responsible for the performance of all aspects of the organization.

Component. EA components are those plug-and-play resources that provide capabilities at each level of the framework. Examples include strategic goals and measures; business services; information flows and data objects; information systems, web services, and software applications; voice/data/video networks, and associated cable plants.

Composite. An EA artifact that uses several documentation modeling techniques and/or represents several types of EA components.

Configuration Management. The process of managing updates to EA components and artifacts, ensuring that standards are being followed.

Convergence (technology). The tendency for technologies that were originally unrelated to become more closely integrated and even unified as they advance.

Crosscutting Component. An EA component that serves several lines of business. Examples include email systems that serve the whole enterprise, and financial systems that serve several lines of business.

Cryptocurrency. A digital currency, which is an alternative form of payment created using encryption algorithms.

Culture. The beliefs, customs, values, structure, normative rules, and material traits of a social organization. Culture is evident in many aspects of how an organization functions.

Current View. An EA artifact that represents an EA component or process that currently exists in the enterprise.

Data. Data items refer to an elementary description of things, events, activities, and transactions that are recorded, classified, and stored, but not organized to convey any specific meaning. Data items can be numeric, alphabetic, figures, sounds, or images. A database consists of stored data items organized for retrieval.

Data Domain. The middle of five hierarchical layers in the Holistic EA Framework that contains data/information related assets and activities.

Data Migration. The process of assessing, improving, and moving a data collection from one database to another via standard formats/methods.

Deal. "The deal" refers to the legal contract to acquire an organization.

Due Diligence. The process of analyzing certain characteristics of something. In the case of M&A, this refers to the analysis of the structure and function of another organization with an eye on possible acquisition.

Enterprise. An organization or sub-activity whose boundary is defined by commonly held goals, processes, and resources. This includes whole organizations in the public, private, or non-profit sectors, part(s) of an organization such as business units, programs, and systems, or part(s) of multiple organizations such as consortia and supply chains.

Enterprise Architecture (EA). The analysis and documentation of an enterprise in its current and future states from an integrated strategy, business, and technology perspective.

Executive Sponsor. The executive who has decision-making authority over the EA program who provides resources and senior leadership for the program.

Framework. The EA framework is a structure for organizing information that defines the scope of the architecture - what the EA program will document and the relationship of various areas of the architecture.

Governance. A group of policies, decision-making procedures, and management processes that work together to enable the effective planning and oversight of activities and resources.

Horizontal Component. A horizontal (or crosscutting) component is a changeable goal, process, program, or resource that serves several lines of business. Examples include email and administrative support systems that serve the whole enterprise.

Hyperconvergence. The use of a single vendor's hardware and software products to create an integrated, software-defined data compute, storage, and network platform.

Information. Information is data that have been organized so that they have meaning and value to the recipient. The recipient interprets the meaning and draws conclusions and implications.

Information Technology. A type of resource that supports the creation, analysis, sharing, archiving, and/or deletion of data and information throughout an enterprise.

Infrastructure Domain. The bottom level of the five hierarchical layers in the Holistic EA Framework that contains facilities and networks.

Internet of Things. The globally interconnected grid of voice, data, and video networks that host end-user (edge) devices for people and organizations.

Knowledge. Knowledge consists of data or information that have been organized and processed to convey understanding, experience, accumulated learning, and expertise as they apply to a current problem or activity.

Knowledge Warehouse. A knowledge warehouse is the component of an enterprise's knowledge management system where knowledge is developed, stored, organized, processed, and disseminated.

Kubernetes. An open-source system for automating deployment, scaling, and management of containerized applications.

Line of Business. A distinct area of activity within the enterprise. It may involve the manufacture of certain products, the provision of services, or internal administrative functions. Also known as a segment.

Machine Learning. Algorithms and statistical models that computers use to perform a task without instructions by relying on patterns and inference.

Merger. The brining together of two organizations.

Mergers and Acquisitions (M&A). The purchase of an organization by another organization and subsequent restructuring of both into one.

Methodology. The EA methodology defines how EA documentation will be developed, archived, and used, including the selection of a framework, modeling tools, and on-line repository.

Mission Statement: A succinct description of why the enterprise exists.

Network: A connected set of facilities, equipment, and transmission media/waves that enable the exchange of voice, data, or video signals.

Performance Gap. An identified activity or capability that is lacking within the enterprise, which causes the enterprise to perform below desired levels or not achieve strategic or tactical goals.

Program. An ongoing activity that manages existing processes/resources or oversees development of new processes/resources via projects.

Project. A temporary endeavor undertaken to create a unique product, service, or result.

Restructuring. The process of changing the structure and functions of two organizations as they are brought together.

Robotic Process Automation. The use of software robots (bots) to re-design and improve the speed and effectiveness of business processes.

Segment. A line of business.

Stakeholder. Everyone who is or will be affected by a program, activity, or resource. Stakeholders for the EA program includes sponsors, architects, program managers, users, and support staff.

Strategic Domain. The top level of the hierarchical Holistic EA Framework that contains the organization's goals and objectives.

System. A type of EA component that is comprised of hardware, and software, and activities that has inputs and outputs.

Systems Domain. The fourth of five hierarchical levels of the Holistic EA Framework that contains system and application assets and activities.

Vertical Component. An EA component that is contained within one line of business. Examples include a system, application, database, network, or website that serves one line of business.

Virtualization. Software applications that emulate hardware devices, logically partition operating systems, or manage applications as groups.

Vision Statement. Succinctly describes the competitive strategy of the enterprise.

Appendix B

The HEA Framework

This appendix describes the structure and purpose of the Holistic EA6 (Cube) Framework that is used in this book. The Holistic EA analysis and documentation process is accomplished through an EA implementation method that includes (1) the framework, (2) components, (3) current architectural views, (4) future architectural views, a plan for managing the ongoing transition between these views, and vertical threads that effect the architecture at all levels.

Analysis and documentation, as organized through an EA framework, provides standardized, hierarchical views of the enterprise from an integrated strategy, business, and technology perspective, shown below.

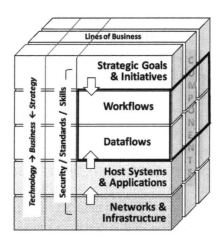

The Origin of Frameworks

IT modelling and documentation frameworks emerged during the era of mainframe computing as data, software, and hardware requirements became more complex and multifaceted, and as the types of end-users increased and their locations became more distant. Reflecting the nature of that era, most early architectures were technically oriented, often vendor and/or product specific. Vendors of software and hardware products increasingly touted their own proprietary solutions, standards, and product lines under the banner of information or systems architectures. While this vendor-driven approach to architecture did serve to advance the capability of computing in general, it also created significant incompatibility problems for enterprises that operated many IT products from multiple vendors.

In addition to the issue of product incompatibility, there was a focus on developing and operating individual information systems versus the creation of an overall IT capability within an enterprise. Furthermore, systems-level IT planning grew out of an approach to analysis and design that focused on meeting a specific set of requirements within the enterprise. For example, many enterprises introduced IT in response to a perceived need for automated support for accounting, payroll, and administrative business functions. This often grew to include manufacturing, service, and sales support. In most cases, each of these business requirements were met by individual system solutions based on proprietary vendor approaches and products. The result was a heterogeneous collection of IT resources that independently supported business areas but could not exchange information outside of a particular system or business area. It was this scenario that gave rise to terms like "stovepipe systems" and "islands of computing capability."

This scenario was increasingly problematic to enterprises that sought to share information between lines of business and support functions. Further, the duplication in systems capability and cost of operating and maintaining a myriad of independent systems became a focal point for improvement. A desire to create interoperability, reduce costs, and increase capability was the organizational driver that changed things.

During the mid-1970's and 1980's this change came in two main areas: database and network design. First, an approach to information systems analysis and design that was based on the enterprise's information requirements came about through the introduction of standardized methods for modelling data, structure, and process. Second, the era of distributed client-server computing came into being as "dumb" mainframe terminals began to be replaced by "smart" desktop computers that could be networked in a client-server design that reached throughout an enterprise.

In the first area, an approach to database design, now known as the "structured" approach, was developed for modelling the processing and structure of data. Data Flow Diagramming (DFD) techniques allowed enterprises to identify how an information system would process data in support of a business function. The Entity-Relationship Diagram (ERD) technique allowed analysts to identify the types of data items that an enterprise wanted to collect along with the attributes and relationships of those data items. Through these two analysis methods, enterprises could design more efficient and capable "relational" databases that used procedural programming languages (e.g., COBOL, FORTRAN, C) which were capable of serving multiple information systems and business processes. Further, this shifted the analysis and design focus from proprietary solutions to generic information requirements.

In the second area, the movement from mainframe to distributed computing also served to change the way that information systems and networks were designed. While structured information modelling techniques promoted new relational database designs, networked computing promoted the hosting of these databases in multiple locations on smaller computer "servers" that could be located closer to the end-user. Information systems standards based on international and industry agreements emerged, as did new designs for the hosting and transport of the information. Important examples include the Open Systems Interconnection (OSI) Reference Model for information networks that was proposed by J.D. Day and H. Zimmerman in 1983. This model has seven layers that address services, interfaces, and protocols. Prior to that, in 1974 the Transport Communications Protocol (TCP) was proposed by Vinton Cerf and Robert Kahn that led to work on a private research network that connected universities and selected military and business enterprises throughout the nation (known as the ARPANET). In 1978, version of TCP was split into two inter-related protocol sets, one for data communications and another for inter-network (internet) addressing – the Internet Protocol (IP). The acceptance of TCP/IP on a broad scale in the late 1980's and early 1990's promoted the integration of telecommunications and data network infrastructures and provided the catalyst for the dramatic growth of the global Internet. Other standards for data transfer emerged in the late 1980's and early 1990's including a standard that defined "Ethernet" local area networks and Asynchronous

Transport Mode (ATM) networks that promoted integrated voice, data, and video.

Data hosting also changed as developments in computer microprocessors, hard drive storage, removable disk storage, and telecommunications interfaces all made the desktop computer, also known as the personal computer (PC), a viable candidate to support print, file, and application hosting functions. Since the early 1980's the performance capability of PCs has risen dramatically each year, while the cost of PCs has dropped. This dynamic boosted the movement away from mainframe computing to networked computing based on 'client' and 'server' PCs working together to share data and applications. Standardized approaches to application development began to emerge as a result, along with protracted competitive battles among vendors to develop products that would dominate in the new networked and converged computing environment.

The early 1990's also saw the introduction of a new approach to designing databases. Focusing on the problem of separating structure from process in modelling relational databases, an "object-oriented" approach was developed that took advantage of new programming languages (i.e., Java, C++) that could support data objects that had attributes and behaviours. Additionally, these data objects could encapsulate (prohibit changes to) certain areas of their code to protect them from alteration. This was significant in that objects then represented reusable code whose quality in key areas was assured. Finally, the non-encapsulated areas of code offered users the ability to customize or add attributes and behaviours such that objects became a building block for application and database development.

It was during this time that some of the first writing on information architecture frameworks began to emerge. In 1987, Dennis Mulryan and Richard Nolan (he later developed the Balanced Scorecard) wrote about "Undertaking and Architecture Program" and in 1991 Brandt Allen and Andrew Boynton wrote an article entitled "Information Architecture: In Search of Efficient Flexibility." In 1987 and 1992, John Zachman published seminal articles in the IBM Systems Journal about an idea for an Information Systems Architecture (ISA) that used a matrix to hierarchically organize business and technology documentation to identify what, how, where, by whom, when, and why were processes occurring.

The Zachman ISA Framework

In the late-1980's John Zachman observed that the data processing requirements of many of his IBM clients were becoming more complex. There was a need to show information systems from several perspectives that addressed this complexity and promoted planning, design, and configuration management. Zachman drew from both the aircraft and construction industries in developing a highly intuitive and comprehensive schema for documenting information systems architecture (ISA) in the context of several hierarchical perspectives characteristics. Zachman's ISA framework is a schema with rows and columns that functions much like a relational database in that he calls for the development of basic or "primitive" architectural artifacts for each of the 30 cells in the schema, such that none of these artifacts are repeated in other cells or combined to create what Zachman calls "composite" products. By documenting the ISA (now known as the Zachman EA Framework) in detail at each level of the EA framework, an enterprise develops multiple views of their processes and resources that are useful to senior executives, line managers, and support staff. Further, Zachman's approach addresses what, how, where, who, when, and why questions about an enterprise. The Zachman Framework for EA (v3.0) is shown below:

	What	How	Where	Who	When	Why	
Executive Perspective (Planners)	Inventory Identification	Process Identification	Distribution Identification	Responsibility Identification	Timing Identification	Motivation Identification	Scope Contexts
Management Perspective (Owners)	Inventory Definition	Process Definition	Distribution Definition	Responsibility Definition	Timing Definition	Motivation Definition	Business Concepts
Architect Perspective (Designers)	Inventory Representation	Process Representation	Distribution Representation	Responsibility Representation	Timing Representation	Motivation Representation	System Logic
Engineer Perspective (Builders)	Inventory Specification	Process Specification	Distribution Specification	Responsibility Specification	Timing Specification	Motivation Specification	Technology Physics
Technician Perspective (Implementers)	Inventory Configuration	Process Configuration	Distribution Configuration	Responsibility Configuration	Timing Configuration	Motivation Configuration	Tool Components
Enterprise Perspective (Users)	Inventory Instantiations	Process Instantiations	Distribution Instantiations	Responsibility Instantiations	Timing Instantiations	Motivation Instantiations	Operational Instances
	Inventory Sets	Process Flows	Networks	Assignments	Timing Cycles	Incentives	

Since 1992, John Zachman has gone on to influence a number of different EA frameworks and writings on the EA, including the author's initial EA6 and current EA6 frameworks, as well as this textbook. While Zachman's basic ISA approach is evident in his current schema, many new concepts have been addressed such as how IT security is an implicit element in each cell's artifact(s). Zachman has written a number of papers that are available through his website on how his approach to EA addresses a number of old and new issues and how it is used in current work with organizations worldwide.

The Spewak EA Planning Method (1992)

About the time that John Zachman was releasing his second article to expand the original ISA Framework, Steven Spewak was further extending these ideas into a planning-oriented framework that incorporated new features including a focus on business, an implementation approach that includes principles and values, a migration strategy, and ties to project management. Spewak was the Chief Architect for DHL Systems Inc. at the time of developing his "Enterprise Architecture Planning" (EAP) method. He was also the first person to prominently feature the term "enterprise" in his framework as a way to emphasize the need for architecture to move beyond individual systems planning. Spewak's definition of the term architecture is as follows:

"Since the aim of EAP is to enable an enterprise to share data, the term enterprise should include all areas that need to share substantial amounts of data. A good and proper scope for enterprise often equates to a business unit, division, or subsidiary because such enterprise units include all of the business functions for providing products and services to customers. Also, with responsibility and control of the bottom line, the economic benefits and justification of EAP can more easily be established".

Dr. Spewak stated that EAP is a method for developing the top two levels of Zachman's Framework. The seven phases of EAP are grouped into a four- layer "wedding cake" shaped model that crates an implementation sequence, as is shown below.

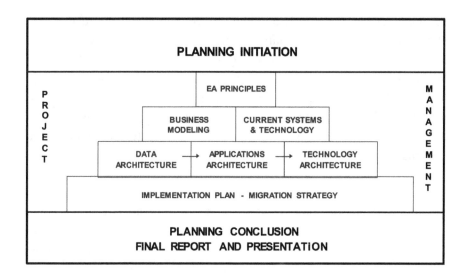

The Open Group EA Framework (TOGAF) (1995)

The TOGAF approach is suitable for developing specific solutions at the business, data, or systems levels of the EA6 Holistic Framework. It originally focused on the development and maintenance of mainframe computers and associated data centers (known as the C4ISR). Since then, it has evolved into an eleven-step method.

The EA3 and EA6 Frameworks (2004 and 2020)

This book uses holistic, generalized framework for EA analysis and design that can be used with any type of large, complex organization in the public, private, or non-profit sectors. Developed by Scott Bernard in 2003 and originally called the EA3 "Cube" Framework, various elements were drawn from the work of Talcott Parsons, James Thompson, John Zachman, Steven Spewak, the Federal EA Framework, and the Department of Defense Architecture Framework. The EA3 Framework used the generic shape and three visible faces of a cube to illustrate the close relationship between the structure, functional domains, and service areas of an organization. The framework was introduced as one of the six basic elements of a complete

EA approach (see Chapter 1), and highlighted the hierarchical relationship of five sub-architecture domains (strategy, business, data, systems, and infrastructure) and three "threads" (security, standards, and skills) that touch each domain. The idea of consistent scaling was also introduced (cubes within cubes) to promote the documentation of organizational sub-units using the same methods, so that you can decompose EA views from overviews to individual systems, or you can aggregate consistently from systems, programs, business units, to the entire organization.

In 2017, Bernard began developing EA concepts to support organizational mergers and acquisitions (M&A) and for use in an EA professional certification curriculum that he has taught at Carnegie Mellon University since 2005. Bernard renamed the framework "EA6 Cube" and brought the other three faces into play (culture, value, and risk) to support the focus of pre-deal analytic due-diligence and post-deal restructuring.

Enterprises can implement the EA6 HEA Framework directly or can use it as an initial baseline for the development of their own EA management and documentation approach. Many enterprises will most likely need to modify certain elements of the EA6 Framework to fit their particular needs, which is encouraged as it is recognized that business, government, military, non-profit, and academic enterprises have different cultures, economic drivers, and critical success factors. These differences may require adjustments in the framework in order to best implement an EA program that captures the current and future business and technology environment.

Common characteristics of most EA frameworks that the EA6 Framework also captures are that they address multiple, often hierarchical views of the enterprise and technology, and that they support integrated systems planning and implementation. The EA6 Framework serves primarily to organize IT resource planning and documentation activities. The framework is hierarchical to distinguish high-level views that are of value to executives and planners from the more detailed views that are of value to line managers and staff.

The sub-architectural areas covered at each level are arranged to position high-level strategic goals at the top, general business services and information flows in the middle, and specific support applications and the network infrastructure at the bottom. In this way alignment can be shown between strategy, information, and technology, which aids planning.

Goals and Initiatives. This is the driving force behind the architecture. The top level of the EA6 Framework identifies the strategic direction, goals, and initiatives of the enterprise and provides clear descriptions of the contribution that IT will make in achieving these goals. Strategic planning begins with a clear statement of the enterprise's purpose and/or mission, complimented by a succinct statement of the vision for success. This is followed by descriptions of the strategic direction the enterprise is taking, scenarios that could occur, as well as the competitive strategy that will ensure not only survivability, but success in terms that the enterprise must define. These overarching statements are then supported through the identification of goals and supporting initiatives that include measurable outcomes and metrics.

Workflows. (Products and Services) This is the architecture's intended area of primary influence. The second level of the EA6 Framework identifies the business products service workflows of the enterprise and the contribution of technology to support those processes. The term 'business service' is used to mean processes and procedures that accomplish the mission and purpose of the enterprise, whether that is to compete in the private sector, provide public services, educate, provide medical services, or provide a defense capability. Strategic planning helps to direct and prioritize the various business services and product delivery activities in an enterprise to ensure that they are collectively moving the enterprise in the strategic direction that is set out in the Strategic Plan. Business services then need to be modelled in their current state and if change is anticipated, also modelled in the envisioned future state. Business services and product delivery processes should be eliminated if they are not adding sufficient value to the enterprise's strategic goals and initiatives. Business services and product delivery activities should be modified if change can increase value to the enterprise, be it a minor adjustment or a major shift in how that activity is accomplished. Technology is often a key enabling element in increasing value but should not be the driving factor in the reengineering or improvement of business services and product delivery processes. It is important to review and adjust the process before IT is applied to ensure that optimal value and efficiency are achieved.

Dataflows. Optimizing data and information exchanges is the secondary purpose of the architecture. The third level of the EA6 Framework is intended to document how information is currently being used by the enterprise and how future information flows would look. This level can be reflected through an IT Strategy document that ties into the enterprise's Strategic Plan and/or Business Plan. The purpose of the IT strategy is to establish a high-level approach for gathering, storing, transforming, and disseminating information throughout the enterprise. The use of concepts such as knowledge management, data mining, information warehouses, data marts, and web portals can be organized through the IT strategy. The design and functioning of databases throughout the enterprise are also documented at this level as are standards and formats for data, data dictionaries, and repositories for reusable data objects.

Systems and Applications. The fourth level of the EA6 Framework is intended to organize and document the current group of information systems, and applications that the enterprise uses to deliver IT capabilities. Depending on changes at the upper levels of the EA6 framework (Business services or Information Flows) there may be planned changes to systems/ applications that must be reflected in the architecture's future views. This area of the EA6 framework is also where components are a prominent feature in service-oriented architectures, as increasingly interoperable commercial applications are available to enterprises (e.g., J2EE and .NET industry standards). Large, modular applications can handle entire lines of business and/or back-office functions (i.e., financial systems, manufacturing control systems, and supply chain management systems). Often referred to as Enterprise Resource Planning (ERP) systems, these commercial applications may offer modules of functionality that can be customized to allow an enterprise to reduce the overall number of applications that they operate and maintain. While ERP systems rarely provide all of the functionality that an enterprise needs for business functions and administrative support, this modular approach is reflective of a "plug- and-play" strategy that enterprises can adopt at this level of the EA6 Framework to increase interoperability and reduce costs.

Networks and Infrastructure. This is the connectivity grid of the architecture, the host environment for applications and systems. The fifth and bottom level of the EA6 Framework is intended to organize and document current and future views of the voice, data, and video networks that the enterprise uses to host systems, applications, websites, and databases. This level also documents the infrastructure of the enterprise (e.g. buildings, server rooms, capital equipment). Local Area Networks (LANs), Wide Area Networks (WANs), System Application Networks (SANs), Intranets, Extranets, Wireless Networks, Mobile Networks, and Computing Clouds are documented at this level so that efficient designs can be implemented through the future architecture that reduce duplication, increase cost and performance efficiency, and promote availability and survivability. Often, an enterprise will determine that certain IT capabilities are critical to the success of the enterprise, and in these areas the architecture should reflect redundant resources in different locations such that these capabilities could continue to be available if the primary resource became unavailable.

Lines of Business within the EA6 Framework

A Line of Business (LoB) is a distinct area of activity within the enterprise. LoB can also be referred to as 'vertical' mission areas or a "segment", which may involve provision of services, product development/delivery, or internal administrative functions. Each LoB has a complete architecture that includes all five hierarchical levels of the EA6 Framework. The LoB therefore can in some ways standalone architecturally within the enterprise, except that duplication in data, applications, and network functions would occur if each LOB were truly independent, and crosscutting activities that reduce this duplication would not be represented. There may be cases where an enterprise would want to incrementally develop their EA due to cost or other considerations, and architecting individual LOBs is one way to do this. The LoB architectures then must be tied together so that the EA correctly represents the entire enterprise, which is needed for the EA to be of maximum value to executives, management, and staff.

Crosscutting Components within the EA6 Framework

To avoid the inefficiencies of duplicative support within LoBs, crosscutting business and technology components are established to provide common service and product delivery capabilities, databases, application suites, and network infrastructures. Crosscutting services are aimed at reducing application hosting costs, increasing the sharing of information, and enabling enterprise-wide infrastructure solutions. Examples of crosscutting initiatives include email service, administrative services, telephone service, video teleconferencing facilities, and computer server rooms.

Planning Threads within the EA6 Framework

EA documentation includes "threads" of common activity that pervade all levels of the framework. These threads include security, standards, and workforce considerations.

Security. Security is most effective when it is an integral part of the EA management program and documentation methodology. A comprehensive security and privacy program have several focal areas including information, personnel, operations, and facilities. To be effective, IT security must work across all levels of the EA framework and within all of the EA components. One of the most important functions of the EA is that it provides technology-related standards at all levels of the EA framework. The EA should draw on accepted international, National, and industry standards in order to promote the use of non-proprietary commercial solutions in EA components. This in turn enhances the integration of EA components, as well as better supporting the switch-out of components when needed.

Skills. One of the greatest resources that an enterprise has is its people. It is therefore important to ensure that staffing, skill, and training requirements are identified at each level of the EA framework, and appropriate solutions are reflected in the future architecture. A Workforce Plan (Human Capital Plan) is perhaps the best way to articulate how human capital will be employed in enabling technology capabilities, which underlie business services and information flows.

Six Faces of the EA6 Framework

The faces of the EA6 Framework are arranged in terms of the relationship to each other, the hierarchy of sub-architecture domains, and the grouping of lines of business. The five levels of the framework are hierarchical and integrated so that separate sub-architectures are not needed, as shown below.

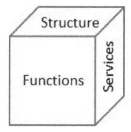 

The following are the general topics and content on each face of the HEA Cube Framework:

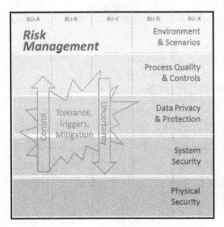

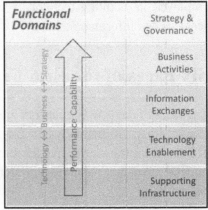

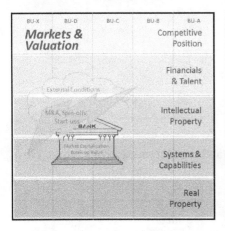

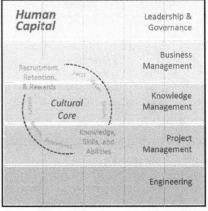

The information that is gathered in each face area should use industry best practices and be correlated using concepts presented in this book and my other book *An Introduction to Enterprise Architecture* (4th Edition, ISBN 1728358051).

The diagram on the next page is suitable to make a paper cutout, with the sides taped together to form a cube. This may provide additional insight as to how the cube framework organizes the information on each face that has a relationship to the adjacent faces and domain areas.

Organizational Structure

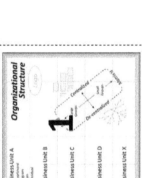

1

Business Unit A
- Department
- Program
- Team
- Individual

Business Unit B

Business Unit C

Business Unit D

Business Unit X

Functional Domains

4

Strategy & Governance

Business Activities

Information Exchanges

Technology Enablement

Supporting Infrastructure

Performance Capability

Technology ↔ Business ↔ Strategy

Risk Management

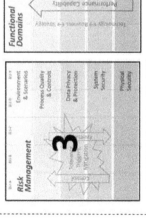

3

Environment & Scenarios

Process Quality & Controls

Data Privacy & Protection

System Security

Physical Security

Products & Services

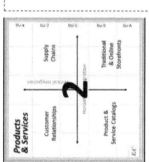

2

BU-X BU-D BU-C BU-B BU-A

Supply Chains

Customer Relationships

Traditional & Online Storefronts

Product & Service Catalogs

Vertical Integration

Horizontal Integration

Markets & Valuation

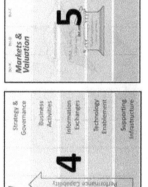

5

BU-X BU-D BU-C BU-B BU-A

Competitive Position

Financials & Talent

Intellectual Property

Systems & Capabilities

Real Property

Human Capital

6

Cultural Core

Leadership & Governance

Business Management

Knowledge Management

Project Management

Engineering

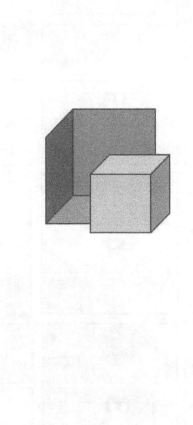

Printed in the USA
CPSIA information can be obtained
at www.ICGtesting.com
LVHW040044080824
787683LV00030B/308